Meeting God at a Dead End

Meeting God at a Dead End

Discovering Heaven's Best
When Life Closes In

Ron Mehl

MULTNOMAH BOOKS ◆ SISTERS, OREGON

MEETING GOD AT A DEAD END
published by Multnomah Books
a part of the Questar publishing family

© 1996 by Ron Mehl

International Standard Book Number: 0-88070-932-4

Cover design by David Carlson
Cover illustration by Stefano Vitale

Printed in the United States of America

Most Scripture quotations are from:
The New King James Version (NKJV)
© 1984 by Thomas Nelson, Inc.

Also quoted:
The Holy Bible, New International Version (NIV)
© 1973, 1984 by International Bible Society,
used by permission of Zondervan Publishing House

The King James Version (KJV)

The New Testament in Modern English, Revised Edition (Phillips)
© 1972 by J. B. Phillips

The Modern Language Bible (MLB)
The Berkeley Version
© 1945, 1959, 1969 by the Zondervan Publishing House

For information:
QUESTAR PUBLISHERS, INC.
POST OFFICE BOX 1720
SISTERS, OREGON 97759

96 97 98 99 00 01 02 03 — 10 9 8 7 6 5 4 3 2 1

Dedicated to my mom, whom I dearly love,
and who, from the Scriptures and the example of her life,
has taught me that with God there are no dead ends.

Edith Swanson

1922—1995

Contents

Acknowledgments   ix

1   Once upon a Dead End   11

2   God's Waiting Room   35

3   Too Tired to Care   55

4   Baby Steps on the Waves   75

5   Run Home!   93

6   The Great Intruder   111

7   A Man with No Hands   131

8   Waking Up on a Dead End   149

9   "Lord, What Am I Doing Here?"   169

10   The Last "At Bat"   191

11   The Mark of the King   209

12   The Final Dead End   229

I will be forever grateful for the people who have helped to make this book a reality.

With deep appreciation, I acknowledge the professionalism, love, and plain old hard work that characterizes the entire staff of Questar Publishers. Your encouragement and support have touched me greatly.

I am extremely thankful to the congregation, council, staff, and pastors of the church I serve, for their prayers, sacrifice, and dedication to ministry, which has made my life so easy.

To our son Ron Jr., whose gift of writing has helped me in so many ways.

Special thanks to Rev. Chuck Updike whose spiritual insights have added so much to my life. And to Dr. N. M. Van Cleave and Dr. Raymond Cox for their suggestions. And to the memory of Dr. Roy Hicks Jr., whose friendship, love, and experiences have so greatly influenced my life and this book.

Finally, I am grateful for Larry Libby. He is a friend I highly regard and has become a mentor and teacher when it comes to writing. When I grow up, I want to be able to write just like him. He's a gifted craftsman when it comes to words. Whenever I've come to a dead end, and that's pretty often, he's always there to show me the way out. My life is richer because of him.

Chapter One

ONCE UPON A DEAD END

For two frightened, hurting, young men, it looked very much like a dead end.

Neither thought he could go much further. Neither knew what to do. Both realized — without admitting it out loud — that they might not live through the night.

Jonah, a high-school graduate from our church, was badly wounded. He had a severe concussion, and his arm was shattered with a grisly compound fracture — jagged bone piercing the skin. Both ankles were injured: the right one fractured, the left with torn ligaments. The temperature on the side of the mountain was dropping rapidly, and their light clothing was soaked clear through.

But worst of all was the darkness. A tranquil sea of stars burning silently overhead only seemed to mock their predicament. They needed better illumination than pale starlight to scale the seventy-degree incline of an icy mountainside! One false step might send them plunging into the darkness below. Again.

They had to decide. To go further seemed foolish — perhaps deadly. But staying where they were was no solution at all. Jonah needed medical help — fast. And dressed the way they were, they would die of exposure. Which was preferable...

a quick death or a slow one? Billy didn't know what to do, and Jonah was so badly injured he could hardly speak for himself. It was on Billy's shoulders — a heavy load for an eighteen-year-old. *What should he do? Which way should he turn?*

"I–I don't think we're gonna make it," Billy told Jonah, shivering. "I don't think we can go any further. We can't see. It's just too dark."

If they could see, they had at least a slim chance of getting out alive. But without light — well, it didn't seem much use. Then Billy saw something that made no sense at all. A soft glow seemed to be radiating out of Jonah's midsection.

"What's that?"

⁓

Terror fell suddenly on that bright Sunday afternoon, near the end of the last leg of the boys' last summer outing.

Earlier in the day, the six high-school buddies had set out to conquer the 10,495-foot summit of Mount Jefferson in the Oregon Cascades. Besides Jonah and Billy, the climbing party included Chris, Dan, Jake, and Ben. Eric, not feeling well, had decided to remain at base camp. All of the boys were eighteen, except for Ben, who was still seventeen.

Just weeks before, the inseparable friends had graduated from Aloha High School in Beaverton, Oregon. Each had set his sights on a different college. But they all wanted one last glorious adventure — together — before they went their separate ways.

When you're eighteen, you look ahead and see open doors and green lights and wide highways stretching off into the hazy distance of the future.

When you're eighteen, climbing mountain peaks looks like the easy and natural thing to do.

When you're eighteen, you never think about the possibility of running into a dead end.

A little after three o'clock on that July afternoon, the boys were about four hundred feet from the summit. Just four hundred more steps through rock and snow and they would stand together at that dazzling pinnacle. From the top they would be able to look north and see Mount Hood, Mount Adams, Mount St. Helens, and Mount Rainier. To the south they could count on seeing the Three Sisters towering nearby, the skiers' favorite — Mount Bachelor — and perhaps even Mount Shasta, shimmering on the southern horizon.

But it wasn't to be. Not on this trip. Not on this day. As he glanced up at the summit looming just ahead of him, Chris accidentally dislodged a large rock that went crashing down the mountain. Chris yelled a warning, and Jonah, ten yards below, leaped out of the way — and lost his balance.

Jonah tumbled down the steep incline followed by the rolling boulder. Three quarters of the way down the slope, the rock grazed Jonah's head and knocked him unconscious.

"NO!" Chris yelled. "I killed my friend! *I killed Jonah!*" Then Chris too was sliding down the snowy slope after his friend.

As it turned out, he had a quite a ways to go. Jonah fell over nine hundred feet.

In the fading light of late afternoon, he lay in a crumpled heap at the bottom of a deep ravine creasing the side of the mountain. Logically, no one could have survived such a fall. After all, people die from falls off bicycles, falls down a few concrete stairs, or falls from the top of stepladders. A fall of nine feet can kill you. A fall of ninety feet is nearly always fatal. *How could anyone fall nine hundred feet and live?*

Chris stopped his own slide just inches from the edge of the crevasse where his friend was lying. As he clambered down the shaley slope, he thought — just for a moment — that he'd heard the sweetest sound imaginable. But it couldn't be…could it? *Yes!* Jonah had moaned! *He was alive.* His left arm had snapped like a matchstick, and his face was a mask of blood. But he was alive!

Slowly the others picked their way toward the ravine, white faced, wide eyed. After a quick huddle Chris and Jake were dispatched back to the trailhead to find help. Ben, Dan, and Billy would wait with Jonah.

But what would they *do* with Jonah? Everyone could feel the temperature drop as the sun slipped lower on the horizon. That's the way it is at those elevations. No matter how warm the day, darkness brings winter. The boys' light summer attire — shorts and fleece pullovers — wouldn't be much help when the mercury plunged below freezing.

Slowly, painfully, they began to move toward the safety of camp. Ben and Dan decided to hurry on ahead, planning to return to meet Billy and Jonah with warm clothes and food.

Jonah could hardly walk. There were stretches on that terrible climb back up the steep slope where Billy had to get behind Jonah, put the top of his head on Jonah's backside, and use his wrestler's strength to push him up the incline.

Most of the time it was just step after agonizing step, swinging ice axes and pulling themselves up inch by inch, foot by foot.

Then Jonah's ice ax missed contact, and he fell.

Grabbing hold of each other, the boys slid down a long snowfield — straight toward the churning waters of Milk Creek below. As he was sliding, Billy thought he could stop himself. But he knew he could never stop both of them. What should he do? Wouldn't it be better to save at least one life?

No way! If Jonah was going to die, then Billy wanted to die along with him. He let himself fall.

They flew over the bank of the creek, hit a rock midstream, and spun out of each other's grasp. Billy hit his head on the rock and felt his body twist in the rushing water. Jonah swept by, heading toward a waterfall. Billy screamed as his friend shot by him and out of sight. Then, as he struggled for footing in the water, he saw Jonah's upraised hand downstream, reaching for a better hold. Jonah was still alive! He had been wedged behind a rock, just a few feet from the top of the falls.

Billy and Jonah crawled from the stream dripping wet and numb with cold. Darkness had descended; an inky, wilderness night hid the way back to safety. They still needed to get back to camp, but now — in addition to the cold and darkness — they faced yet another obstacle: Jonah had injured both ankles in the river.

Now what? How much could two kids survive? As they staggered away from Milk Creek, Billy began seriously to wonder if they would ever make it back. Wouldn't it be wiser to wait — and hope for the best? Yes, they might lose their hands and feet to frostbite, but wouldn't that be better than losing their lives in another fall?

"Maybe…maybe we should stay down here and wait it out," Billy told Jonah.

"Whassa matter?" Jonah mumbled through cracked and swollen lips. "You a wimp or somethin'?"

"I–I don't think we're gonna make it. I don't think we can go any further. We can't see. It's just too dark."

That was the moment Billy saw a glow shining from his friend's midsection.

"What's that?" Billy shouted. "What's that — in your pocket?"

"Oh!" said Jonah, staring dazedly at the gentle radiance beneath his wet pullover. "It's my flashlight!"

Jonah had forgotten about the small flashlight tucked in his front pocket. Somehow it too had survived the nine-hundred-foot plunge down the mountain and the subsequent tumble into the stream. And now, it had seemingly switched itself on.

This is from God, Billy thought to himself. *He's saying, "You're going to make it, and I'll show you the way."*

Jonah, too, took it as a sign. He knew the Lord had sent it to give them hope and help to carry on. They had to keep moving, keep climbing. And somehow they did. At half past two in the morning, the pair stumbled back into camp to await their rescuers.[1]

Some of God's miracles are huge and earthshaking, lighting up the sky. Others are quiet and tiny. Something as small as a weak moan at the bottom of an icy crevasse. Something as tiny as a glow of light at the last moment on a dark dead end.

My young friend Jonah had no doubt about it. Shortly after he came out of surgery at University Hospital in Portland, I went to visit him. Both of his feet were wrapped, his arm was in traction, and his face was bruised and swollen almost beyond recognition. A couple of IVs dripped essential fluids into his veins.

Even though he spoke through a fog of medication, Jonah couldn't stop talking about God. Thanking Him. Praising Him. He knew he shouldn't be alive. Knew it wasn't some stroke of extraordinary luck that had saved him. Knew it wasn't because he and Billy had been jocks, or tough-minded kids, or whatever else the news media had said. They could call it luck or pluck or whatever they wanted to. Jonah was very well aware that he was still alive because of the grace and mercy of God.

Jonah had come to the darkest night of his young life and found God there, waiting for him at the dead end.

Sitting there by his bedside at University Hospital, watching him drift in and out of sleep, I'd like to have told him he'd never have to face another dead end. But I knew better. No, I'm no prophet, and I can't see into the future. But I know this: If Jonah is going to walk with God through his years, mature in his faith, and grow in his love for the King of kings, there'll be other such dead ends this side of heaven. Plenty of them.

> ...Somewhere along the line a young woman may awaken a love in his heart he never knew he possessed...and break his heart in a way he never dreamed it could be broken.

> ...At some point in his life he may find himself in a financial emergency...with absolutely no prospects and no idea where to turn.

> ...Someday he may be standing by his mailbox, holding a long-awaited letter from a medical school...denying him entrance.

> ...Some morning in the middle of his years, he may wake up and feel an overwhelming revulsion for his job, his life...and an overpowering desire to run.

> ...Some still night he may be leaning over the stainless-steel railing of a crib in the soft light of a hospital nursery...willing a tiny baby to live.

...Some gray afternoon he may find himself
staring at the wall tiles in a narrow, sterile
examining room...trying to wrap reality
around a doctor's grim prognosis.

...Some dark hour before dawn he may be star-
ing into a cup of black coffee...waiting for word
about a teenager who hasn't come home.

Jonah learned something about the grace and timing and strength and mercy of the Lord on the cold, unforgiving slopes of Mount Jefferson. He and Billy had come to a dead end, had no one to turn to but God, and found out that God was enough.

That's what a dead end in this passage called "Christian life" is all about. It's about coming smack up against a brick wall and seeing no gates whatsoever — or even any loose bricks. It's about coming to the end of our wisdom, the end of our strength, the end of our ideas, the end of our options, the end of our coping skills, and the end of our cherished dreams. It's about standing in that dark, hopeless place and discovering — beyond all logic, against all hope — that God is very much alive and can fill our little cup to overflowing.

David, who learned most of his theology sitting at dead-end roads, said it like this:

*If I say, Surely the darkness shall cover me; even
the night shall be light about me. Yea, the darkness hideth not from thee; but the night shineth
as the day: the darkness and the light are both
alike to thee.* (Psalm 139:11–12, KJV)

Chances are, young Jonah's dead end was more dramatic than yours or mine will ever be. Not everyone falls nine hundred feet down the side of a mountain, and climbs out of a crevasse, only to fall again into a river — and lives to chat about it over a cup of cocoa. Your dead ends may never make the evening news or a two-page spread in the newspaper as Jonah's did. Folks around you may not give your predicament a second glance. *But your dead ends are big enough to you.* You may not have a concussion, two broken ankles, or a shattered arm...but then again, you might willingly trade those injuries for what you're feeling inside. What's a compound fracture compared to a broken heart? As Solomon wrote: "a broken spirit dries the bones.... Who can bear a broken spirit?" (Proverbs 17:22; 18:14).

Your dead end — whatever it is and wherever it might be — is the worst! Yes, you say, that kid fell almost a thousand feet off a mountain into a deep crevasse, and that was bad. But I'll take that anytime over what I'm facing now. My teenager — the apple of my eye — just told me she's pregnant...*give me the crevasse!* My wife of twenty-five years has been diagnosed with breast cancer...*give me that fall off the mountain!* My forty-five-year-old husband just lost his job and slipped into a depression...*I'd rather endure a broken arm!* My dead end hurts, too! My dead end seems dark and hopeless, too.

And while we're on the subject, can you tell me this?

If God loves me, why does He *allow* dead ends in my life? Why does He bring me to those crazy cul-de-sacs where I don't know where to go, don't know which way to turn, and don't know what to do?

I can't help but be reminded of a time when poor old Moses had about two million people asking him the same question.

The nation of Israel had just walked away from four centuries of national slavery in Egypt. Moses' directions from the Lord were clear. He had been instructed to lead that huge, harried throng to the very edge of the Red Sea. In the meantime, however, Pharaoh was having second thoughts about letting this amazingly useful labor pool just slip over the border. What in the world had he been thinking of? He decided to call out his army and bring the Israelites back — or kill them, just on principle.

Back in the wilderness, it didn't take God's people long to realize they had been neatly delivered into a dead end.

Pharaoh's mighty chariot force was thundering down on them from one side, and the impossible depths of the sea stretched before them on the other.

Evidently, there had been some serious miscalculation here. Or...had there?

> *And when Pharaoh drew near, the children of*
> *Israel lifted their eyes, and behold, the Egyptians*
> *marched after them. So they were very afraid,*
> *and the children of Israel cried out to the LORD.*
> *Then they said to Moses, "Because there were no*
> *graves in Egypt, have you taken us away to die*
> *in the wilderness? Why have you so dealt with*
> *us, to bring us up out of Egypt?... For it would*
> *have been better for us to serve the Egyptians*
> *than that we should die in the wilderness."*
> (Exodus 14:10–12)

It's significant to note that Israel hadn't just blundered into this desert dead end. Pharaoh certainly thought that was the case. According to his calculations, "They are bewildered by the land; the wilderness has closed them in" (Exodus 14:3). But Pharaoh was dead wrong. His former slaves had been *led* into the desert, cut off by the sea.

In the old Westerns fast-riding outlaws fleeing the posse

would sometimes find themselves trapped in one of those infamous "box canyons." But for the Israelites this was no wrong turn at the pass. God had told Moses exactly where to set up camp. And now here they were. Completely trapped. Utterly helpless. Destruction on one side, doom on the other. There was absolutely nowhere left for them to turn. Nowhere to look but up.

Which was precisely where God wanted them to be.

> *Moses said to the people, "Do not be afraid.*
> *Stand still, and see the salvation of the LORD,*
> *which He will accomplish for you today. For the*
> *Egyptians whom you see today, you shall see*
> *again no more forever. The LORD will fight for*
> *you, and you shall hold your peace." (vv. 13–14)*

The point is, Israel was supposed to *learn* something from that dead end — something they couldn't learn in any other way. They could have never learned it from a book. They could have never learned it from a sermon. It was something they needed to experience. Moses told them to keep calm, keep quiet, stand steady, take a deep breath…and watch what was about to happen. This was one instance when the best counsel was "Don't just do something, stand there!" God Himself was about to do something that had never been done before. He was about to show His power in a way none of them could have imagined or dreamed.

After they had passed safely through, on the other side of the sea the Israelites watched the mighty walls of water collapse on the pursuing Egyptian army, and their hearts were filled with wonder and awe.

> *Thus Israel saw the great work which the LORD*
> *had done in Egypt; so the people feared the*
> *LORD, and believed the LORD and His servant*
> *Moses.* (Exodus 14:31)

On the other side, after it was all over, after they had discovered that God had opened a back door in their dead end, everyone suddenly felt like singing.

> *"Your right hand, O LORD,*
> > *was majestic in power.*
> *Your right hand, O LORD,*
> > *shattered the enemy.*
> *In the greatness of your majesty*
> > *you threw down those who opposed you.*
> *You unleashed your burning anger;*
> > *it consumed them like stubble....*
> *Who among the gods is like you, O LORD?*
> > *Who is like you —*

majestic in holiness,

awesome in glory,

working wonders?"

Exodus 15:6–7, 11, NIV

Where had they learned such things about this God of their fathers? Where had they learned He was majestic in power? How had they discovered He was majestic in holiness? Who told them He was awesome in glory? When had they gotten the idea He was a wonder-working God, like no other?

They didn't read about it or hear about it. They weren't singing hymns out of someone else's dusty old hymnbook. They had experienced all this for themselves…at a dead end.

If it hadn't been for their frightening impasse at the Red Sea, they would have never really known these things.

No, their newfound knowledge and faith didn't carry them very far down the road (about as far as the next dead end). Nevertheless, their deliverance that day would be celebrated *forever.* Their wide-eyed little boys and girls learned about the power and grace of God through this incident. So did their grandchildren, great-grandchildren, and great-great-grandchildren. Some five hundred years later, the psalmist would sing of the event, leading all Israel in a mighty chorus of praise.

He saved them for His name's sake,

That He might make His mighty power known.

He rebuked the Red Sea also, and it dried up;

So He led them through the depths,

As through the wilderness....

Then they believed His words;

They sang His praise.

Psalm 106:8–9, 12

A few centuries after that, in a time of national rebellion, Isaiah called out:

"Where is He who brought them up out of the

sea

With the shepherd of His flock?

Where is He who put His Holy Spirit within

them,

Who led them by the right hand of Moses,

With His glorious arm,

Dividing the water before them

To make for Himself an everlasting name?"

Isaiah 63:11–12

God gained great glory at that desert dead end, and His people learned that what mattered most was following Him and trusting Him with all their hearts.

Wasn't the end result *worth* that dead end, no matter how unnerving it might have been? And — when you boil it all down — isn't that what life is all about, anyway? Isn't that why we're here on planet earth?

Maybe you and I have never faced a situation just like that, but let's admit it, we live in a world of dead ends. It's been that way since Adam and Eve turned their backs on their Creator and went their own way. Human experience has been, is, and always will be filled with dead ends, blind alleys, box canyons, and washed-out bridges.

I think about that sometimes when I drive on the two-level Marquam Bridge in Portland, high over the wide Willamette River. As you're heading east, you can't help but notice how one of the lanes, sealed off with concrete barricades, juts straight out into nowhere. Back in the midsixties freeway engineers constructed the bridge that way so it could eventually link up with an on-ramp from the proposed Mount Hood Highway.

But there is no Mount Hood Highway — and may never be. Somewhere along the line, for some reason now forgotten, the idea died. But there's that lane, projecting into midair, ever so ready for a road that will never be. It makes me think about our condition as fallen men and women. We have grand ideas, great dreams, and soaring hopes. But so many of our plans end in frustration and failure. So many ambitious roads end at impassable barricades — or drop off suddenly into empty space.

If you haven't faced a dead end lately, you will. That's not doom-and-gloom talk; that's *life*.

And in every one of these dead ends we feel like we're going to die! Just a few miles from the scene of their dramatic rescue at the Red Sea, the Israelites ran out of food in the desert. They cried aloud, "You have brought us out into this wilderness to kill this whole assembly with hunger" (Exodus 16:3). Right! As if God would blow a thoroughfare through the middle of the sea only to let them all die of malnutrition just a few miles down the road!

Speaking about that moment, the psalmist notes:

> *They soon forgot His works;*
> *They did not wait for His counsel.*
>
> Psalm 106:13

But really…we're just like them, aren't we?

We, too, forget His works.

We, too, forget to wait for His counsel.

Spinning our wheels in some frustrating dead end, we find ourselves overwhelmed. Anxious. Angry. Depressed. Stressed to the edge. *"Oh God, how did I get here? What's happening? Help! I'm not going to make it! I'm not going to sur-vive! There's no way out! Why did You bring me to this dead end to let me die?"*

Circumstances rage around us. Emotions scream within us — or fall dead flat so that we can't feel anything at all. It's hard to get your perspective or remember much of anything in a dead end.

You might *think* you have your spiritual act together, and you might assure yourself that you "know enough" about God. But until you run into a dead end, you really don't know what you know. As the anxiety and frustration rise, you forget all your pat formulas, handy acrostics, and memory verses. All the sermon outlines you've heard over the past year go clean out of your head. Nothing makes sense. It's dark. It hurts. Fear settles in like a fog.

So what do you do?

Well…if you can manage to remember only one thing, *remember to look for God at your dead end.* He will always be there.

Up on Mt. Jefferson, Jonah and Billy were badly shaken. They were hurting, scared, cold, and disoriented. It was hard to think straight. It was so dark they couldn't see. But in the worst moment, when their lives hung in the balance, a tiny light blinked on under Jonah's shirt. The Almighty God of the universe who holds endless suns and countless galaxies in His hand winked at them through a three-volt flashlight. In that faint little glow, two boys remembered God, took courage, and climbed to safety.

This is a book about little lights on dark dead ends. No, the light may not show up right away. It may appear after a long season of darkness. You may have to first discover that you really *are* at a dead end. It's an old law of human nature that as long as we can cope on our own, we will. As long as we can figure it out, we'll wear out our brains with the effort. As long as we can dig under a wall using our fingernails, toenails, and teeth, we'll break our hearts trying. Knowing this, He may let us wait awhile at that dead end, until our hearts learn to wait on Him. He may have to give us enough time to realize that, apart from Him, there really is no hope.

For some of us, the dead ends must be severe. It may *take* a nine-hundred-foot fall. For others of us, a deep disappointment might do it…or even an unquenchable inner longing that refuses any resolution short of God Himself. God is sovereign, and He knows what it will take to open our eyes.

As you leaf through the pages of Scripture, you see two kinds of people. There are those who come to these dead ends, cry out to God, and move on into greater usefulness and a deeper walk with Him. And there are also those who come to dead ends and *stay there* — or destroy themselves trying to scale an unscalable wall.

One thing you can know about your dead end, no matter how dark, no matter how frustrating, no matter how frightening: *God is there.* God is waiting at your dead end. And if you will call out to Him, if you will wait on Him, if you will watch for Him and "stand still," He will show you something of Himself that you would never see otherwise.

The plain fact is, we'll never catch a glimpse of the "majestic power," "majestic holiness" and "awesome glory" of our God and Savior until we come flat up against an immovable barrier or an unyielding obstacle. If it weren't for dead ends, we would enjoy a smooth, bland, unruffled passage through life...all the way to hell.

But God loves us enough to bring us to the end of ourselves. And when you finally meet Him at your dead end, you may find it wasn't a dead end at all. It was the very road your heart longed for all along.

---

[1] For the chronology of these events, I am indebted to the excellent article by Antje Spethmann in the August 31, 1995, issue of *The Oregonian.*

Chapter Two

GOD'S WAITING ROOM

Waiting does not number among "my favorite things."

Just recently Joyce and I were thinking back to the birth of our firstborn. I was recalling all the hours I had to spend in the waiting room, marking time until this little person decided to show up.

We had checked Joyce into the hospital early one evening, and Ron Jr. chose not to make his grand entrance until 4:30 the next afternoon. That's a long wait by most anyone's standards. Yes, I realize Joyce had to wait, too, but at least she had something to do! She had *work* to do, something to keep her mind occupied, and all those fresh-faced nurses bringing her snacks, rubbing her back, and fluffing up her pillow.

I'll clue you, there weren't any fresh faces or fluffy pillows where *I* was. I was stuck out in a smoke-polluted waiting room with a bunch of nervous, bristly-faced men who needed a shower and an attitude adjustment. I don't remember one of those guys offering to rub my back. This, of course, was back in the days of complete segregation, the women in one part of the hospital (being coddled and pampered), and the men all bunched together in a stuffy little waiting room with seven-year-old issues of *House Beautiful* and *Woman's Day*.

Nowadays, of course, the whole family and all the friends

and neighbors come into the delivery room with tape recorders, video cams, pizzas, and those funny foil balloons. It's a party!

I've never been in a pool hall, but I got a better idea of what they might be like after that long vigil in the waiting room. It was pretty grim. The guys chain-smoked cigarettes before the baby was born, and big cigars afterwards. As I waited, it seemed like seven different men came in, got the Big Announcement, shook hands all around, and walked out grinning.

What in the world was Joyce doing in there? I was impatient but also worried sick.

Leafing through an ancient, yellowed *Reader's Digest,* I'd just begun my third reread of an article — "Ten Steps to Organizing Your Life" — when I heard a baby screaming at close range. A nurse brought the unhappy little package into the room in her arms, and it was howling full tilt.

I jabbed the man next to me and said, "There you go. That one must be yours." But the nurse walked over to me and said, "Mr. Mehl, this is your little boy."

It was my neighbor's turn to jab *me* in the ribs. "There must be some mistake," I told her. "Our child wouldn't act like this." The little fella was all red, wrinkled, and bald as a billiard ball.

It had been quite a wait. But at least in that case…it was worth it.

Waiting doesn't always seem quite so productive. Yet if you've ventured very far at all into this segment called adulthood, you've probably come to realize that it is a rather large and mostly unavoidable chunk of life. When we're small, we're waiting to grow a little taller, impatiently eying Mom's pencil marks on the wall. When we're in elementary school, we're waiting for the adult sophistication of junior high. In junior high, we realize that high school was what we were *really* waiting for. In high school, we're waiting for a car, college, marriage, or that first "big money" job. And on it goes.

We wait for service in restaurants, counting the holes in the top of the salt shaker. We wait for the traffic to edge forward an inch or two on the way home. We show up fifteen minutes early for our doctor's appointment and end up waiting forty-five minutes — just to get into one of those chilly little examining rooms where we wait *another* half-hour in our underwear.

God has a waiting room, too, you know.

You might not find those exact words in Scripture, but it's there all right. From one end of the Book to the other, God has brought His people into the waiting room of delayed dreams.

Can you picture it...that great, celestial waiting room? Can you see it in your mind's eye? One very large room stretching out both ways farther than you can see. Shining floors, marble walls, white-shaded lamps…and countless people sitting in chairs, glancing now and again at the clock on the wall, clearing their throats, drumming their fingers, chewing their lips…and waiting.

Waiting for God to respond.

Waiting for God to keep His promise.

Waiting for God to speak.

Waiting for God to answer.

Waiting for God to heal.

Waiting for God to act.

A large poster on the wall reads, "HOW LONG, O LORD?"

Can you imagine yourself sitting there…in God's waiting room? You look over to your left and there's Noah, calmly thumbing through a boating magazine. He's waiting for something called "rain." He's never seen it before, but God had said it would come — a lot of it.

Over on your right is Abraham. He's been there a very long time, waiting for a little son whose name would be "Laughter." He's become an old man in that waiting room, but he'll stick it out. He has a promise in his pocket with God's signature on it.

Job is there, too, so weak and doubled over with pain and

sorrow he can barely stay in his chair. He's waiting for healing, waiting for a few encouraging words, waiting for someone to help him make sense of a life shattered into a thousand jagged pieces.

Ruth's there, too, waiting for a husband — and a redeemer.

David is there, of course, waiting for a promised kingdom. If you listen carefully, you can hear him pray…

> *In the morning, O LORD, you hear my voice;*
>> *in the morning I lay my requests before you*
>> *and wait in expectation.*

> Psalm 5:3, NIV

Thin, gaunt-faced Jeremiah sits beside him, quietly weeping, wiping tears on the cuff of his ragged robe. He's waiting for some sign of hope that his empty, burned-out city will ever again echo with the sounds of laughter, song, and worship of the true God.

One striking young man sits with his hands folded in his lap, his expression alternating between intense longing and sturdy, determined patience. His name is Joseph, and he has spent some of the prime years of his life right here, in God's waiting room.

TESTED BY THE WORD

Joseph's case is so celebrated that Israel wrote it into their national hymnbook, for all generations to sing and bless the Lord. Here's the way it's written in Psalm 105:

> *Moreover [God] called for a famine in the land;*
> *He destroyed all the provision of bread.*
> *He sent a man before them —*
> *Joseph — who was sold as a slave.*
> *They hurt his feet with fetters,*
> *He was laid in irons.*
> *Until the time that his word came to pass,*
> *The word of the LORD tested him.*
>
> Psalm 105:16–19

Have you ever been tested by the Lord, waiting for the promises of His Word?

You probably remember Joseph's story from the Book of Genesis. He was sold by his jealous brothers into Egyptian slavery, falsely accused by his master's wife, and thrown into the subbasement of an Egyptian prison. You can tell the story in a couple of sentences, but how do you put into words the loss of those precious years? He was probably sixteen or seventeen when he was captured, and possibly *thirty* before he was released. Before he stepped out into the light and fresh air of freedom, his youth had come and gone. An irretrievable part of his life had slipped away.

That's a long time to spend in a waiting room.

That's a long time to spend parked on a dead end.

And what of those dreams God had given him as a boy? What about those whispered promises of leadership and honor and greatness? Would they ever come true?

He would learn, of course, that God was still at work in his life — in ways vastly beyond those boyhood dreams of his. Oh, but the waiting was hard! Bitterly hard.

Psalm 105:18 says,

> *They bruised his feet with shackles,*
>
> *his neck was put in irons.* (NIV)

My dear friend Luis Palau quotes an old English translation of the last part of that verse that says: *"The iron was burnt into his soul."*

In other words, God was molding Joseph during those lonely years, forging him into a man of steel. Through all the injustice and waiting he had to endure, the iron was burning into his soul. Joseph had to become a strong and durable man before God could use him in the great ways He had in mind.

While Joseph's dreams were on hold, God was working.

He was working in Israel. He was working in the courts of

Egypt. He was working with the weather patterns encircling the globe. He was working in the hearts of Joseph's brothers. And He was working in Joseph's heart, too, refining the young man's faith, drawing him ever closer to the heart of God. Even though Joseph's plans, hopes, and dreams were waiting, God was *not* waiting. Joseph was at a dead end, but God was not. He was working ceaselessly on His servant's behalf.

At the end of many years, Joseph could reflect on those long days and years of waiting and hardship his brothers had put him through, look into their eyes, and say from the heart, "You meant evil against me; but God meant it for good…to save many people alive" (Genesis 50:20). Jacob, prophesying in the power of the Holy Spirit shortly before his death, said this of his son Joseph:

> *Joseph is a fruitful bough,*
> *A fruitful bough by a well;*
> *His branches run over the wall.*
> *The archers have bitterly grieved him,*
> *Shot at him and hated him.*
> *But his bow remained in strength,*
> *And the arms of his hands were made strong*
> *By the hands of the Mighty God of Jacob.*
>
> Genesis 49:22–24

Where did that fruit in his life come from? How did he remain victorious even in the face of unfair treatment, cruelty, and hostility? Where did he get his steadiness and strength? Where did he get that iron grip that held tight to God's promises?

He found them in God's waiting room.

At some dead ends there is an immediate response when we cry out to God. Our dreams are put on hold — but only for a little while. Before we know it, God has thrown the way wide open again, and we're enjoying fulfillment, healing, and peace. But in the mysteries of His ways, it doesn't always happen like that. There are times when you will have to wait…in that place of weakness…in that place of uncertainty…in that place of loneliness or pressure or pain…and it may seem like a long time before the way opens up for you again.

It was that way for Carol…a lady who spent a great deal of time in God's waiting room.

THE LONGEST WAIT

In spite of everything, Heather drifted further and further away.

In spite of all the love and tenderness, in spite of the many attempts at discipline, in spite of all the pleading and prayers and tears, Heather became increasingly estranged from her little family.

For Carol, Heather's godly single mother, it was exactly like living a nightmare.

It was like one of those dreams where you desperately long to speak to someone who's walking rapidly away from you. You try to call out, but you can't speak. You try to run to catch up, but your feet seem encased in concrete, and you can't move. And that person who somehow owns so much of your heart keeps walking and walking into the distance, fading into the horizon.

As the months of her teenage years went by, Heather became more and more rebellious, more and more hard. Finally she moved out altogether. Carol knew her daughter was living a wild, promiscuous life and had become deeply involved with drugs.

The little girl who had chattered nonstop, played with Barbies, and could light up a room with her smile was gone. This was a Heather that Carol scarcely recognized. Dark rings encircled her eyes, and thick makeup could not mask her pallor. She wore her hair in a strange, chopped-off punk style and dressed in army surplus.

But her mother loved her and prayed every day for her salvation.

Down on her knees beside her bed in the dark, when she ought to have been sleeping before another long day of work, Carol poured out her heart. "Lord, I know where my daughter is. I know what she's doing, and I know how she's living. But I know You love her, Lord, and because I know You love her, I'm going to rest in Your faithfulness — to save her, minister to her, touch her, redeem her, restore her."

So she prayed.

But nothing happened.

Carol wept until she had no more tears and cried out to the Lord morning and night. But there was no change. No softening. No remorse. Nothing.

Eventually Heather moved to a different city, and Carol lost contact altogether. Friends who had the courage to speak of the matter urged Carol to let her go. To concentrate on the other kids. To think about herself a little. Heather was too far gone, they told her. There was no hope.

And as the weeks became months, and the months became years, it began to look as though they were right.

But still, her mother prayed. Still, her mother hoped.

Finally there was no need to pray any longer. Word came that Heather was dead.

It fell to Carol to go to Heather's little apartment in a run-down part of a nearby town and collect her daughter's meager possessions. Her heart felt like a stone as she drove the rainy streets, searching for the address, knowing there would be no one home. The rain continued to fall as she stood at the door, fumbling with the key they had sent her. She had never set foot in this place before. What would she find? Would she be able to bear it? *What more could she have done?* She had prayed so fervently for her daughter's restoration...for her salvation.

And now it was too late for prayer. It was out of her hands. Maybe it always had been.

The apartment was cold and dark, but its condition wasn't as bad as she had feared it might be. It hurt to see how Heather had lived in her last days, how impoverished she had been. But even though the apartment was drab and the furnishings sparse, there was a neatness that surprised Carol. The place had been recently cleaned.

Scanning the room, Carol's eye was caught by a white envelope on a little desk in a corner. It was an unstamped, unsent letter in Heather's familiar hand.

And it was addressed to Carol.

Feeling suddenly weak, she slumped down into a chair. Her fingers trembled as she opened the envelope and unfolded the letter. It was penned on plain binder paper and dated shortly before her girl's death.

Dear Mom:

   I just wanted you to know that I'm coming home next weekend.

   Mom, I have news for you. I just received Jesus Christ as my Savior. He's changed my life, and I'm so thankful. And Mom — to think that you would love me during those days and years when I was such a mess — when I was everything but what a mother would want her daughter to be — to think that you would love me and stand with me and care for me has meant more to me than you'll ever know.

   I can't wait until next weekend when we can sit together and I can hug you and tell you just how much I love you and how much you mean to me.[1]

There was a little more, but Carol's eyes were streaming with tears. She bent over the desk as the rain pattered on the windows and wept as she had not wept before.

The old nightmare had been a lie. She *would* catch up with her girl one day. They would walk together and laugh together again, in a better place.

Most people would have given up on Heather. But the Holy Spirit doesn't give up on people. Sometimes you come to those dead ends where you get so tired of waiting you want to throw in the towel. But He never does. You want to quit, but He keeps on faithfully pursuing.

You may even come to the point where you find yourself saying, "I can't carry on anymore. I can't believe or trust anymore. In my own strength and in my own wisdom I have nothing left to hope." It's at that point — while clinging with all your strength to God — that you move to another dimension of faith, beyond what seems logical, beyond what makes sense. You find yourself trusting God at a new level. More than ever, He *becomes* your hope.

But what's going to keep you there? What's going to keep you waiting on Him? It's the promise of God.

ANNA'S HOPE

To me, the little story of Anna has always been one of the most tender, neglected portions of the Christmas story.

Do you remember the scene? Joseph and Mary had come into the temple in Jerusalem to present their firstborn to the God of Israel and make a sacrifice for Him as the law required. While they were walking through the temple courts, a very old woman approached them, almost as if she had been waiting for them. And there must have been something about her eyes...

*Now there was one, Anna, a prophetess, the
daughter of Phanuel, of the tribe of Asher. She
was of a great age, and had lived with a husband
seven years from her virginity; and this woman
was a widow of about eighty-four years, who did
not depart from the temple, but served God with
fastings and prayers night and day. And coming
in that instant she gave thanks to the Lord, and
spoke of Him to all those who looked for redemp-
tion in Jerusalem.* (Luke 2:36–38)

Though Scripture doesn't say so, I imagine this dear old widow taking the baby Jesus in her frail arms and lifting her face to bless the Lord. I can picture a shaft of morning light reaching her through the pillars of the temple, touching her as she held Jesus and praised God.

Here was a woman who spent virtually her whole life in God's waiting room. After seven years as a wife and home-maker, the Lord took her young husband from her side. For the rest of her life, until age eighty-four, she stayed in the temple, fasting and praying. Surely she was one of those faith-ful Jews who was waiting, waiting, waiting for God's Messiah. Perhaps, like the old man Simeon that Luke spoke of a few verses earlier, she'd had some word from the Lord that she would actually live to see His coming.

Year after year, decade after decade she stayed in the temple, fasting and praying, perhaps prophesying of the coming Messiah. But nothing happened. Nothing changed. Everything went on as before. There were no results.

People probably begin to snicker. "Lady, your life is going by. You'd better get about the business of really living."

But she stayed on as the years slipped past. By that time she must have seemed like part of the temple furniture. "Hey, isn't that the same lady who was prophesying in my grandfather's time? Don't tell me she's still at it!"

To all outward appearances, this was a lady at a dead end. This was a woman whose life stalled out early on and never got back on track. There were probably those who clucked their tongues and said, "What a shame. Think of all the opportunities in life she's missed. What good does she really imagine she's doing?"

Who could have realized that she would meet *God* at that dead end?

Who could have predicted that she would cradle the King of the Universe in her arms?

Who could have guessed that she would gaze into the very eyes of God's Messiah?

As it turned out, she was in God's waiting room all those years waiting for a Baby! And when He came, she was in the right place at the right time to proclaim Him and His mission to all the faithful hearts in the city of Jerusalem. Her message was no longer simply, "The Redeemer is coming." Now she could add, *"And I have seen Him!"*

And what about the impact of her life? How many people around the world do you suppose have read the Gospel of Luke during two thousand years of history? How many people have read her name and pondered her story? Millions? Billions? The Holy Spirit in His sovereignty chose to honor her life in the pages of eternal Scripture. Somehow, in God's mighty providence, Anna's life reaches down through the centuries and millennia to touch you and me. That's impact!

The lesson is, don't worry if God has kept you in His waiting room. Let *Him* worry about your life impact. If He has you there, He knows how to use you! Even if the world never sees, He may be using you to demonstrate something to the invisible principalities and powers, as He did with His servant Job.

Be faithful, wait on Him, and you will affect the future in ways you can't comprehend. Trust Him for it! Hang onto what God has shown you and told you — even when you find yourself at a frustrating dead end. The people who really survived the dead ends of Scripture were those who clung in faith to the *reality* of what God had said.

Joseph held on through his youth…and became the ruler of Egypt.

Anna held on for a lifetime…and met God face to face.

What promise are you clinging to in His waiting room? When the hours get long, when the magazines get old, and when the smoke gets thick, you need a strong hope and a strong promise to give you endurance and keep your anticipation alive.

David, who paced plenty of his own waiting rooms in his time, may have said it better than anyone:

> *Wait on the LORD;*
> *Be of good courage,*
> *And He shall strengthen your heart;*
> *Wait, I say, on the LORD!*
>
> Psalm 27:14

---

[1] To the best of my memory, this was the wording of the letter.

Chapter Three

TOO TIRED TO CARE

I n my younger days when I first moved to Portland and entered the pastorate, I tried to keep in shape by going to the Jewish Community Center across town to play some hoops. I showed up on Monday, Wednesday, and Friday evenings to shoot around, dribble a little, and maybe play a pickup game or two. It was an enjoyable way to get some exercise, find a little friendly competition, and blow off some pent-up anxiety.

But on one particular Monday night I ended up with more competition than I'd bargained for.

When summer rolls around in the Rose City, the community center hums like a beehive. In those days even the Portland Trailblazers used the facilities as an off-season practice site. They practiced free throws, scrimmaged, and generally tried to keep in NBA fighting trim.

One evening I was down at one end of the court, shooting my favorite jump shot, making lightning drives against imaginary opponents, and generally trying to get my heart rate up a little. I'd just kissed a sweet bank shot off the glass and was getting into position for my patented ten-foot jumper, when I suddenly felt a very large hand on my shoulder. I turned around and found myself staring straight into the numbers of someone's practice jersey. Now I'm six-four and unaccustomed to staring into the chest of a man more than half a foot taller than I am. It was a little unnerving.

"Hi," I said.

"Hello," he boomed. "The name's Rick. Rick Roberson."

Well I knew who he was. What Portlander wouldn't recognize the starting center for the Portland Trailblazers?

"Say," he said, "I was watching you, and it looks like you can shoot and handle the ball pretty well. What's your name, anyway?"

"It's Ron. Ron Mehl."

"Where did you play?" he asked. Glancing down, I noticed that he had palmed a basketball in a hand the size of a turkey platter.

"Well," I said, "I played some in Bible college back in —"

He cut me off. "You a preacher?"

"Well…yeah, I am." My answer was a little hesitant. You never know how that revelation will go over.

"Okay," he smiled. "I'll call you 'Preach' then. Now listen, Preach, the other guys are taking a break. How about a quick game of one-on-one?"

I glanced up at his face. *Was he kidding?*

"Uh, sure," I said. "I guess so." I felt like looking around for the *Candid Camera* guy.

"You take the ball first, Preach." He shoved it into my

hands — hands that suddenly felt sweatier than normal.

I looked down at the other end of the court where the rest of the Blazers were cooling off. A few of them had seen Rick talking to me and were looking our way, elbowing each other and grinning.

Okay, Ronnie boy, I said to myself. *This is your big chance. A chance not many guys will ever get in a lifetime. You're about to go one-on-one with a real, live NBA center. Better make it good, kid.*

We faced off against each other at the top of the key. The whole situation still seemed like something out of a silly dream. I made my first move, a little fake to the right meant to take advantage of my smaller size. I really don't know if he was ready or not, but I blew right by him. Shot through with excess adrenaline, I soared a little higher than usual and dunked the ball before Roberson really got off the dime.

From the other end of the court I heard an "Ooooo" and then an "Uh-oh."

Rick looked down from his nearly seven-foot height and smiled again.

"Oh," he said quietly. "So *that's* the way you want to play, is it?"

No, not really, Mr. Roberson. I don't know what got into me. Let's just start over, shall we?

Moving faster than I could have believed for a man his size, he launched himself from the free throw line and just about tore the backboard down as he slammed the ball through the hoop. I no more could have stopped him than I could have held back an eighteen-wheeler with a fly swatter.

There were more "ooos" and "ahs" from down the court...and thus began my relationship with the Blazers of that day.

Just a few days later I was again shooting baskets on one end of the court while some of the Blazers, including Oregon legends Geoff Petrie and Larry Steele, were running drills on the other.

They walked down to my end and said, "Hey, Preach!"

I looked at them, trying to appear casual — like it was every day that a group of NBA guys walked over to shoot the breeze with me.

"Hey, Preach, you wanna play a little three-on-three for conditioning? We need a sixth man, and after watching your one-on-one with Rick the other day, we think you look good enough to keep up."

Now I was really excited. Blood hammered in my temples, and I swallowed hard. The Blazers asked *me* to play full court with them? And what had they said? That I'd looked *good?*

Man, I was proud. I wished Joyce could see me — or some

of the guys from the church. I could imagine what they would be saying when word got around. "Hey, did you know Pastor Ron was working out with the *Trailblazers?* No, I'm not kidding! Hey, we might be looking for a new pastor, guys — they may want to draft him."

The fantasies were pleasant, but I didn't have much time to indulge them. Our scrimmage started out at ninety miles an hour — and accelerated from there.

This definitely wasn't Bible college stuff. It wasn't church league, either. The passes were like artillery shells. The bumps and picks were savage. And I noticed one significant thing right away. *It never stopped.* No one ever stopped to laugh or get a drink or tie a shoe. It was all one nonstop sprint.

After about six times up and down the court, I was gasping like a drowning man. After ten trips, I was experiencing an acute shortage of oxygen, and there wasn't enough of it in the whole gym to satisfy my heaving lungs. I must have sounded like Bill Cosby doing his impressions of a Lamaze class.

It was our turn to in-bound the ball, but Roberson found me in a doorway, backed up against the doorjamb. I was doubled over with my hands resting on my knees.

"Hey, Preach," the big man said. "You all right, man?"

Roberson wasn't even winded. He looked like he might

have strolled to the mailbox and back, sorting through his junk mail.

What made you think I was struggling a little, Rick? Haven't you ever heard anybody breathe this way before? Haven't you ever seen anybody holding up a building before? Haven't you ever seen a guy this shade of purple?

"No — fine — I'm — fine. Just — need — to get — little — water — tha's all."

"Sure, Preach. Take a break."

It was all vain pride, but I didn't want those guys to know how wasted I was. I wanted them to think I was just like them. But as much as I may have wanted to keep up the charade, there was really no hiding it. I simply wasn't in their league. And it wasn't even close.

I made an enlightening discovery that night. When we were all loosening up in the same gym, practicing free throws, taking jumpers, and horsing around, we didn't look that much different from one another. I might have even fooled a couple of people into thinking I belonged on the same court with those guys. But when we got into a *contest*...well, that was a different story. Suddenly it became ridiculously easy to spot the amateur in the bunch.

These men were incredible physical specimens. They worked on their conditioning every day to make themselves the best basketball players in the world. I was only a casual, part-time player at best.

It was a bit of a lesson to me as I collapsed into my car that night in the parking lot. As Christians, we are engaged in a contest with implications beyond our imagination. The stakes are real, extremely high, and the contest never, never stops. It's a simple fact that if we are truly engaged in that contest, heart and soul, we're going to become weary at times. If we're never tired, it probably means we're only playing at being a Christian. Just taking a few shots here and there and dribbling around on the court a couple of times a week.

But if we are truly committed to the battle and running to keep up, we're going to get tired. And that fatigue is a constant reminder that only God can give us the second wind we need to carry on.

NOT QUITE ALONE

A pastor, just like anyone else in his congregation, can feel weak and inadequate at times.

I remember one day when I was particularly tired and weary and felt I had to talk to the Lord about it. I trudged across the parking lot from my office to our worship center and went in to pray.

It was late afternoon, a time when no one else was in the building. It was dark, quiet, and cool in the big auditorium. Perfect praying conditions. I knelt down between the pews, buried my face in my hands, and began to pray out loud, as I like to do sometimes.

"Lord," I said, "I don't want to feel this way. Really — I feel bad about feeling this way. But — well, I just feel like I'm done. I don't think I'm doing all that well. Don't think I'm preaching all that well. Don't think I'm pastoring all that well. Lord — it just doesn't seem to me I'm doing *anything* very well these days. But Lord…it would be nice, really nice if…I mean, I'd just kind of like to know if You're still concerned at all about how I'm doing. It'd be nice to hear from You and have You talk to me once in a while. And maybe You could, You know, just give me a little bit of a reason to believe that You really care — that You're really involved in my life and ministry…"

So I went on with my sad little recitation, complaining a bit maybe, remembering that David got away with it in his psalms.

I'd just about worked myself up into believing I was pretty much alone, abandoned, and washed up when, suddenly, a few yards away from me, a head popped up from between the pews.

It was a little startling. I had to squint into the semidarkness to make sure it really was a head. (But what else would it be?) In a moment I saw that the head was attached to a body — a man's body — because he walked over to my pew and sat down beside me, where I'd been kneeling.

Apparently he'd been down on his knees, too, when I walked in. He, too, had been praying.

And he'd been praying for me.

"Pastor," he said. "I'm terribly sorry to disturb you. Sorry to bother you while you're praying. But, well, I heard you, and I felt like the Lord wanted me to come over and offer to pray for you. I felt like the Lord moved me to come here today — right here — to pray for you. Funny thing is...I really don't know why. You're not the sort of person who seems to need anything. You're so positive all the time. Never seem to need encouragement. But I thought I'd better do what the Lord said and come ask if I could pray for you. I felt like maybe you needed it today."

I nodded, and with that he placed his hand on my shoulder and began to pray that I would experience refreshment and strength in my life, and encouragement in the work of the ministry.

I had been surprised to see that head suddenly pop up out of nowhere in that big, empty auditorium. I had been amazed to learn that — just when I was feeling so weary and alone — someone had been praying for me, only a few yards away.

I guess I shouldn't have been surprised. God knows very well when I'm approaching the end of my strength. Truthfully, He knows it long before I do. And He knows just when to send along an angel or a brother or sister in Christ to fill my empty cup.

It's just what He did for Elijah, when that good prophet had finally reached the end of his tether. Someone popped in on Elijah, too, and taught him what to do at a frustrating dead end called fatigue.

"THE JOURNEY IS TOO MUCH FOR YOU"

And Ahab told Jezebel all that Elijah had done, also how he had executed all the prophets with the sword. Then Jezebel sent a messenger to Elijah, saying, "So let the gods do to me, and more also, if I do not make your life as the life of one of them by tomorrow about this time. And when [Elijah] saw that, he arose and ran for his life, and went to Beersheba, which belongs to Judah, and left his servant there.

But he himself went a day's journey into the

wilderness, and came and sat down under a
broom tree. And he prayed that he might die,
and said, "It is enough! Now, Lord, take my
life, for I am no better than my fathers!"
(1 Kings 19:1–4)

In the previous chapter of 1 Kings, the prophet had performed his mightiest work for the Lord. Standing all alone, he had confronted evil King Ahab and four hundred frantic prophets of the false god Baal. Elijah had called down fire from heaven to consume a sacrifice soaked in gallons of seawater. Then he had personally dispatched all four hundred of the false prophets with the edge of a sword. After that little task, he exercised his faith to the maximum and prophesied to the king that a heavy rainstorm would immediately soak the drought-parched land when there wasn't more than a wisp of a cloud in the sky.

His day's work done, the prophet hiked up his robe and ran over *ninety* miles — from Carmel to Beersheba. (If you'd like to "just do it" yourself on a regulation track in your Nikes, it's 360 laps.) Leaving his equally exhausted servant to gasp for air in Beersheba, Elijah ventured even further into the desert wilderness.

Finally, when he could go no further, he collapsed on the

hot desert sand and crawled on hands and knees to the meager shelter of a desert broom tree. "It's enough!" he told the Lord. "I'm beat. I'm done. Just kill me and be done with it."

The discouraging, self-destructive words pouring from the prophet's parched lips were the voice of his weariness. The Lord knew that and gave his request the consideration it deserved…none at all. Instead of dialoguing with Elijah about it, He simply let the exhausted man sleep.

> *Then as he lay and slept under a broom tree,*
> *suddenly an angel touched him, and said to*
> *him, "Arise and eat." Then he looked, and there*
> *by his head was a cake baked on coals, and a*
> *jar of water. So he ate and drank, and lay*
> *down again. And the angel of the LORD came*
> *back the second time, and touched him, and*
> *said, "Arise and eat, because the journey is too*
> *great for you." So he arose, and ate and drank;*
> *and he went in the strength of that food forty*
> *days and forty nights as far as Horeb, the moun-*
> *tain of God. (vv. 5–8)*

Some people think the answer to fatigue is to start a new Bible study, fast for a few days, and sign up for two new church committees. But in Elijah's case God's prescription was food, water, and lots of rest. The prophet had been doing too much, going too far, and carrying too heavy a load. It was time to pull the plug on all that activity for a while and rest up in Palm Springs.

How unspiritual, you might say. Really? I think it was the most spiritual thing he could have done because it was God who provided him with this season of rest in his life. An angel even came to the prophet, delivering a specially catered meal. (How can you get more spiritual than that?)

How tired was this guy? An angel thumps him on the side to wake him up, serves him lunch, he mumbles "Thanks" and rolls over and goes back to sleep! (Listen, if an angel ever woke *me* up in the morning, I think I'd stay awake for the next six months.) After another forty winks, the angel comes back with Meal #2 and offers counsel every mother in the world would applaud: "Arise and eat, because the journey is too great for you."

What in the world was in those cakes? Talk about power bars! Whatever they contained, it was enough to keep the prophet going strong for the next month and a half, until he'd hiked all the way to the "mountain of God." In other words, *God knew what it would take for Elijah to accomplish the next phase of the journey.* God knew what Elijah needed to accomplish His will.

I think there was a reason for God's delivery truck rolling

up to that bush in the desert. It was to remind Elijah where his true source of strength really lay. It was *God's* provisions he consumed under the broom tree. The cakes were fresh from heaven's bakeries. The water was drawn from heaven's deep wells. And after taking the time to be refreshed by God Himself, the prophet was ready for anything.

Here's the bottom line: When Elijah came to the ragged, tattered end of his strength and endurance, he rested and dined on God. And after he was through resting and dining on God, he had the strength and stamina to step out into a new and exciting phase of ministry.

At Horeb he would meet God in an unusual and powerful way. And shortly after that he would link up with a new friend, ministry partner — and future successor. A young man named Elisha would become as dear as a son to the lonely, battle-scarred prophet.

But please note this: Before any of those significant and life-changing things occurred, Elijah needed to come to a dead end. He wasn't ready to walk straight from the heights of Mt. Carmel to the heights of Mt. Horeb. Even a great and mighty prophet doesn't stride from mountaintop to mountaintop to mountaintop. We are, after all, only human beings with human bodies and human limitations. Even when you're on a tour of mountaintops, there have to be a few valleys in between. And when we come to the end of our strength, when our road seemingly dead-ends in a dry wasteland, it's time to rest and dine on the Lord for a while.

You need a little Wonder Bread from God's own hand.

You need a little living water from the river of God's Spirit.

Jesus said it like this:

> *"Come to me, all you who are weary and bur-dened, and I will give you rest. Take my yoke upon you and learn from me, for I am gentle and humble in heart, and you will find rest for your souls. For my yoke is easy and my burden is light."* (Matthew 11:28–30, NIV)

Elijah had been weary in the ministry — weary in the work of the Lord. But there is another sort of weariness that the Lord cares about, too. It is when we are wearied by our sin and exhausted by going our own direction and pursuing our own desires and trying so hard to meet our own needs.

I believe that's the kind of exhaustion — a weariness of life itself — that the Lord addressed in those words. We're weary from trying to fulfill ourselves, weary from trying to take life into our own hands and make things happen, weary of going it alone. A good definition of sin is simply setting out to meet our own needs in our own way.

The crazy thing is, we'll go *on and on* like that until — in God's tender grace — we finally reach a dead end. Dry, discouraged, and utterly spent, we feel like crawling under a bush and saying, "What's the use? I'm not doing anybody any good. I'd be better off dead."

Once again the message is extremely simple: If you meet God in that dead end of fatigue, it is the best thing that could ever happen on your journey. If, upon realizing you have no resources, you begin to tap into God's provision, you will find strength beyond anything you have ever experienced.

Just as Isaiah told us...

> *He gives power to the weak,*
> *And to those who have no might He increases*
> > *strength.*
> *Even the youths shall faint and be weary,*
> *And the young men shall utterly fall,*
> *But those who wait on the LORD*
> *Shall renew their strength....*

Isaiah 40:29–31

WRONG RACE. . .OR WRONG PACE?

Elijah had told the Lord he wanted to die, that his work was over. But through these circumstances, the Lord was replying to him, "No, you're not done, and you're not going to die. You're going to get some rest. You're going to take some refreshment. And then I'm going to send you some help. From there, we go on... together."

Elijah had thought he was in the wrong race, but the truth was, he'd been running at the wrong pace.

He ran like a scared rabbit to Beersheba and almost killed himself in the effort. But after meeting God and dining on God in that desert cul-de-sac, he *walked* on from there to the mountain of God. And on that mountain, God revealed Himself to His servant in a fresh and profound way.

God didn't want His servant to retire or take an indefinite leave of absence. He just wanted him to set a reasonable, steady pace. Fast enough to get the job done, but slow enough so they might carry on a conversation and keep their relationship intact.

I've heard that one way to judge your pace in a marathon is to run at a speed where you can still carry on brief conversations with fellow runners. If you're running too fast to talk, you're running too fast. You'll burn out before you reach the finish line. It's the same with you and me. If you're running too fast to talk to God through your day, if you're ricocheting like a pinball from one task to another all morning, afternoon, and evening so that you don't even have time to refresh your soul in Christ, you're going too fast. Sooner or later, you're going to dead-end. You're going to collapse in some barren place and crawl under a scraggly broom tree.

At the time, it will seem like the end of the line, the end of your service. In fact, it may signal the beginning of the most productive phase of all.

The fact is, you and I were never intended to run this race solo. The greater the calling, the greater the task, the more you ought to pace yourself, take time to talk with the One who runs beside you, receive His provisions, and rest.

For those who refuse to respond in this way, however, there is a grave spiritual danger. When we are weary and depleted, we are never more vulnerable to the attack of the enemy. Might not Satan have been the source for Elijah's suicidal thoughts in that wilderness? I think so! He had escaped Ahab and Jezebel, but there was another enemy waiting to sink his arrows into Elijah's unprotected flank.

In his letter to weary, suffering believers in the first century, Peter warned them of a dark undertow, waiting to pull their legs out from under them and drag them down. This is how he put it:

> *Be sober, be vigilant; because your adversary the*
> *devil walks about like a roaring lion, seeking*

whom he may devour. Resist him, steadfast in
the faith.... (1 Peter 5:8–9)

He follows with this wonderful encouragement:

And the God of all grace, who called you to his
eternal glory in Christ, after you have suffered a
little while, will himself restore you and make you
strong, firm and steadfast. To him be the power
for ever and ever. Amen. (vv. 10–11, NIV)

If we're not careful, if we're not watchful and vigilant, we may become numb and apathetic in our weariness. We feel an emptiness inside. A vacuum. We can shrug our shoulders and say, "What does it matter?" Then, rather than turning to our only Source of strength, provision, and nourishment, we leave the door open for Satan to gain a foothold...and we're too weak to fight him off or even care.

But just as Peter said, God is in the restoration business. He's got plenty of heavenly cakes, plenty of clear, cool heavenly water, and special places to rest where angels stand guard. "The sun will not smite you by day, nor the moon by night." He knows how to make even the most worn-down and exhausted of His warriors "strong, firm, and steadfast."

His invitation? It's the same as it has always been.

"Come to Me."

Chapter Four

BABY STEPS ON THE WAVES

Whoever tagged Disneyland "the happiest place on earth" never bothered to consult with me.

Call me a kill-joy if you like, but anyone who has ever waited in line for an hour and a half for a one-and-a-half minute ride, or paid half a week's salary for a couple of hot dogs and some *churros*, might appreciate the chance to give a minority report.

Nevertheless…we parents continue to make the pilgrimage to Orange County by the tens of millions every year.

For the children.

For years now one of the park's top attractions has been Space Mountain. The mere mention of the name flutters the hearts and curdles the stomach contents of fathers everywhere. Or at least *this* father. Admittedly I'm somewhat sensitive to heights and motion. I can get a little woozy wearing thick socks. I can get dizzy if I walk around the pulpit too many times while I'm preaching. So just thinking about flying upside down through the smog, clinging to Dumbo's ears, or spinning around in some oversized teacup can move me to fast for a few hours.

Those, of course, were the *old* rides from the fifties. Space

Mountain is another proposition altogether. This isn't just conventional nausea; it's high-tech.

This ride hurtles you through simulated outer space at four hundred miles per hour…negotiates you through ninety-degree corners without slowing down…sends you down nearly vertical drops…and then lets you catch in your lap the lunch you lost at the top of the ride. And why in the world are you doing this?

For the children.

I remember the first time we took our son to Disneyland. He was probably seven or so. Too young, I thought, to grasp the grave error he was committing when he uttered the words, "Come on, Dad, let's ride *Space Mountain!*"

This called for quick strategy. "Listen, Son," I said, taking him aside. "This is serious business. See, Space Mountain isn't just a ride — Son, are you listening? — it's what they call a 'High Speed Turbulent Flume Ride.' Do you know what G-forces are, Son? You do? Well, on this device you pull at least eight or ten Gs. That's more than a Formula One racecar! That's enough to pull the skin back on your face, like a facelift. All right, forget the facelift — that's an adult thing. But Son — look at me, please — you accelerate from zero to sixty in less than 2.3 seconds. This ride defies the laws of physics as we know them. Yes, yes, I see Goofy over there, but listen to me, this is *serious.* This is a ride for adults, for grownups. Did you know they actually created this to train astronauts? Now, your mother and I have taught you to *think.* So — just hold on a minute — are you sure you want to…"

"Hurry up, Dad, the line's getting longer!"

I felt the blood drain from my face. I was sunk. I noticed a sign at the head of the line which specified that people who were pregnant, suffered with back or heart problems, or were not as tall as the bottom of the sign were prohibited from riding. Unfortunately none of those applied to me. At least not *before* the ride. I couldn't vouch for anything after I got off.

The line itself was long, winding, and monotonous. We were sandwiched between the Southern California sun and the heat-baked asphalt. While my son pointed out pictures of moon landings and meteors and chattered about spaceships, my attention wandered. I noticed there were "chicken" exits placed strategically all along the way. If you got halfway through the line and came to your senses, you could still back out. And believe me, I tried to think of a reason — any reason — that might carry weight with my boy. Surely with my adult brain I could outwit a mere child! I fought an overwhelming desire to turn back — the survival instinct runs strong among the Mehls.

What finally did me in was my masculine pride. Bottom

line, I didn't want to look like a wimp in front of my man-child. So I stayed in line. Like a lamb at a slaughterhouse. And why did I do it?

For the children.

Eventually there were no more exits. We were committed. And we were buckled in. Though the ride lasted only minutes, it was hours before I could downgrade the Class Five hurricane in my stomach to a tropical storm.

In retrospect, one thing about the episode — one lingering memory — made it (almost) worthwhile.

It was the way my boy reacted to it all.

I was genuinely surprised to observe that he never became nervous or scared. And he had never faced anything like this before! He had never endured the terrors of space travel. In all his young life since leaving the womb, he'd never been dropped, twisted, shaken, and generally thrown around as he was on that ride. But instead of panicking, he just held tightly onto my hand, wore a wide grin, and kept his confidence intact. No matter what the situation or circumstance, he never displayed the slightest doubt that we'd be okay.

Laser attacks? Alien invasions? Meteor showers? Rapid re-entries? No problem. Just being with his dad was all the assurance he needed.

That was reassuring to me, too. Because I knew that in the

years stretching out ahead of him, there would be bigger drops and tumbles than Space Mountain could ever simulate. There would be lurches, launches, leaps, and lightning turns in life that would make an amusement ride pale by comparison. And through it all, he would need faith and confidence in a Father greater than me.

When the time came…would he trust Him?

More to the point, would I?

Did my confidence and trust in my heavenly Father even match my young son's confidence in me? Before the Disneyland trip, I'd been dealing with a few, potentially frightening, stomach-lurching issues of my own in the ministry. Did it take a wild ride through the darkness with my little boy to show me how far I fell short in my faith?

Peter was probably asking similar questions, after his own wild ride one stormy night.

SECOND THOUGHTS

Jesus, knowing well what the night would hold for His men, sent them across the Sea of Galilee in a boat, saying He would catch up with them later. They thought it was going to be a routine commute to the other side. Jesus knew it was going to be another pop quiz in Faith 101.

But the boat was now in the middle of the sea, tossed by the waves, for the wind was contrary. Now in the fourth watch of the night Jesus went to them, walking on the sea. And when the disciples saw Him walking on the sea, they were troubled, saying, "It is a ghost!" And they cried out for fear. But immediately Jesus spoke to them, saying, "Be of good cheer! It is I; do not be afraid." And Peter answered Him and said, "Lord, if it is You, command me to come to You on the water." So He said, "Come." And when Peter had come down out of the boat, he walked on the water to go to Jesus. But when he saw that the wind was boisterous, he was afraid; and beginning to sink he cried out, saying, "Lord, save me!" And immediately Jesus stretched out His hand and caught him, and said to him, "O you of little faith, why did you doubt?" And when they got into the boat, the wind ceased. (Matthew 14:24–32)

Ultimately, to doubt means to hesitate.

I love what D. L. Moody once wrote about hesitation. "The only mistakes I've made in my life," he said, "were when I took time to think twice." In other words, "I once believed something. I was once convinced of something. I once had no doubt about the rightness of my course. But now…I'm not so sure. Now…well, maybe I'd better think it over a little."

Doubt, I believe, limits God's working in our lives. It impacts what He can do for us and how He can help us. Nevertheless, I do not believe that doubt equals *unbelief.* Unbelief questions God, but doubt questions *me* and God's working in me. Unbelief says, "God, I know what You say You can do, but I can't and won't believe it." Doubt says, "I just can't imagine how God could do such a thing in and through someone like me. I can't comprehend Him using me like that. It's beyond my frame of reference. It overwhelms me!"

God will work with us in our doubts, but He won't tolerate unbelief.

When the Lord speaks about "believing and not doubting in your heart" that God can move a mountain, He isn't speaking about our faith in God's ability. The question for most of us isn't, *Can* God move a mountain? Everybody knows God can move mountains. Of course He can! He made those mountains, so He can move them around like chess pieces anytime He wants to. That's no problem. Where does doubt come in then? Doubt staggers at the thought that He might want to move one through me!

A generation of believers has grown up singing Andraé Crouch's song:

> *Through it all, through it all,*
> *I've learned to trust in Jesus,*
> *I've learned to trust in God....*[1]

But have we? Is that really true?

When the sky is black and the waves are high and we don't see any hope or help on the horizon, have we truly clung to Him and trusted in Him? That's what Peter had to do.

"WHY DID YOU DOUBT?"

Most people read verse 31 and take it as a sharp rebuke, as though Jesus were shaking a stern finger in Peter's face.

> *And immediately Jesus stretched out His hand*
> *and caught him, and said to him, "O you of*
> *little faith, why did you doubt?"*

I don't see it that way. I don't think Christ is saying, "What am I going to do with you? You doubt everything!" I think the Lord is saying, *"I'm coming alongside you because I want to encourage your faith. You were doing so well! Why did you turn back?"*

That, I believe, is what the Lord is about through the days

and moments of our lives. In every situation He's constantly encouraging us to grow, increase in faith, and trust Him more and more. Like a patient, loving Parent, He's helping us to advance from crawling to baby steps...from baby steps to walking...from walking to running with strength and confidence. And in the lives of His disciples, virtually everything the Lord led them to experience in their three-year journey with Him was for one purpose: to develop their capacity for faith.

Far from being the worst doubter on that turbulent night, Peter was leading the way in his faith. Who else climbed out of the boat that night? Who else fixed his eyes on Jesus, squared his shoulders, and started to hike across the waves? Not John. Not James. Not Philip. Not Andrew. It was Peter who threw natural caution into that wild wind and attempted the impossible.

"Lord," he shouted into the gale, "if it's really You, call me over to Your side."

Jesus said, "Come."

And Peter went.

Not *far*, maybe, but my goodness, give the man a little credit. He did walk on water! In those brief, miracle moments, the big fisherman came close — so very close — to entering a whole new phase of life, a whole new phase of belief. He was almost there! But just when he had almost reached that higher plane of walking with Jesus, he hesitated and lost it.

Our Lord's words, "Why did you doubt?" come across to me like, "Oh My child, you were so close! You were within inches of something wonderful! Something that would move you higher and make you stronger! Why did you turn back?"

Peter learned that night that he really did have faith enough to attempt mighty things. But he also learned how much further he had to go. He was growing, yes, but he hadn't arrived yet. His faith was still "little."

I believe that's the reason the Lord allows you and me to come up against those faith-stretching tests and those dead ends of doubt in our lives. He wants to show us how far we have yet to go. He wants to show us we are still of "little faith." It may be we have deceived ourselves along the way. Perhaps we've been telling ourselves that we're a man or woman of great faith. But at that dead end of doubt, staring into the teeth of sheer impossibility, we see how far we really have to go.

At an annual physical checkup we learn where we are in our overall health. A middle-aged friend of mine who wanted to play tennis with his young son went to the doctor to have his sore shoulder checked out. But as they were doing a routine blood pressure check, the doctor said, "Whoa! *Your blood pressure is off the charts!* Did you know that? This is a dangerous situation. We've got to get that down." My friend hadn't dreamed there was a problem. But at that routine checkup, he learned the truth about himself and what he needed to do right away to prevent a heart attack or stroke.

The real issue in his life wasn't tendinitis in his shoulder; it was dangerous, runaway hypertension.

At the dead end of doubt we experience a faith checkup. We find out where we are in our journey of faith. We learn what the *real* issues are in our lives and what we need to do about them.

Some people say Peter didn't have to get wet that night. Maybe so. But then again… *what's wrong* with getting wet as we seek to walk on water? *What's wrong* with going under for a few seconds when the Lord's right there to pull us up again? *What's wrong* with crying out to Him for help and reaching out for His hand? Isn't that better than clinging to our security and not reaching for His hand at all?

Notice that Jesus didn't correct Peter until after He pulled him out of the water. He didn't look down at Peter and say, "Tread water for a while, friend. If you'd get your life together and start repenting and confessing right now, then I might yank you out of that hole." He didn't do that. The Lord helped him out first, got him on his feet, and then they did a little review of what went wrong.

If there was any disappointment in our Lord's voice, I think it was more along these lines: "Peter, I'm so anxious for you to grow into a new level in your faith. I'm so anxious for you to discover how I can use you once you *really* start trusting Me. And, Peter, you already show little flashes of that kind of faith. You're getting closer and closer, but you're not there yet."

The good news of course is that Peter did grow up in his faith. He did stand strong on the Day of Pentecost. He did step into a leadership role in the infant church. He did endure incredible pressure, threats, and persecution. And eventually, he stretched out his arms and let the authorities crucify him, rather than denying his Lord.

Later in his life he wrote: "Cast all your anxiety on him because he cares for you" (1 Peter 5:7, NIV). Where did he learn that truth? He learned it walking in the storm because it was there the Lord encouraged him to carry on.

Don't be too hasty to criticize people who are stepping out in faith and venturing for the Lord — even when they stumble, even when they end up thrashing around with a mouthful of seaweed. It's better than staying in the boat and keeping your feet dry! The only way you're going to grow and mature in your faith is to stand at that place of doubt and fear, reach out your hand toward the Lord's outstretched hand, and take one step — even a baby step — forward.

I don't care how strong you are, you *will* come to the dead end of doubt. Everybody will. As Peter could testify, it's not easy to keep your eyes on the Lord. It's not easy to shut out the distractions and pressures that seek to pull us this way and that. It's not easy to ignore waves and wind and darkness. And I don't care who you are, when you look down and realize that your feet are treading on about three fathoms of turbulent seawater, it's not easy to keep jogging like you were on a sidewalk in the park.

Having doubts is not unspiritual. It's who we are. Even though we look away from our Lord for just a moment, we can lose our perspective and our equilibrium. Sometimes all it takes is a momentary glance — shifting our gaze from the eternal to the temporal — and doubt suddenly floods our heart and chills our soul. Yet when we find ourselves going under, He's still there to grab our hand with a grip that cannot be broken.

GOD'S GYM

There's nothing like a vigorous workout with weights to get the heart pumping and the blood moving, and to make you generally feel a lot better about yourself than you probably deserve to. Until, that is, you take a look around you at all the bulging biceps, triceps, and every other kind of "cep" you can imagine.

It can be more than a little intimidating pumping iron alongside muscle-bound guys in tank tops who *live* for that sort of thing. I remember looking at comic books when I was little that had ads for Charles Atlas bodybuilding stuff on the inside back covers. The ads promised that if you took his course, no bullies would ever kick sand in your face at the beach. Well, we didn't have any beaches to speak of in Bloomington, Minnesota, but we did have bullies. And I thought it would be wonderful to have that "Charles Atlas look" when I grew up.

It didn't quite happen that way. I did fine in sports, but God never saw fit to clothe my slim frame with those rippling muscles that looked so awesome in the ad. So I basically let the bullies go their way, and I went mine.

Even so, when our sons went through serious weight training with their athletic teams, I especially enjoyed watching the trainers help the lifters go through their regimen. You'll see a guy really straining to do five or six repetitions at a certain weight on the bench press machine, and the trainer comes along and drops ten more pounds on the load. Now the lifter is straining just to get the bar off his chest. Then, pushing and trembling and puffing, he manages two or three repetitions.

Why does the trainer do that? To embarrass the man? To overwhelm him? To discourage him? To show him how weak and puny he is? Not at all. If you have a trainer who really cares about his job, he's going to push you a little. He's going to test your limits. He's going to give you goals to work toward and to challenge you until you move up to the next level. Through it all, he creates an environment for you to grow gradually stronger.

I've always thought of faith as a muscle. It needs to be exercised. Stretched. Challenged. It needs to have demands placed upon it on a regular basis so it won't atrophy and wither away.

Running into doubt in your life is like lifting a little more than you're used to. Doubt says, "I'm not sure I can lift that. I think that might be too much for me." Yet the Master Trainer says, "Come on. You've been at the old level too long. You're not growing. Push a little harder and see what you can accomplish."

And truthfully, through faith in Christ and in His power, we can lift more, run longer, climb higher, stretch further, and jump wider obstacles than we might have ever imagined. There is a great deal to accomplish before the King comes back to pull the plug on time and draw us into eternity. And He is ready to equip us for jobs so much bigger than we are...if we'll trust Him.

A B O Y I N A W I N D O W

For whatever reason, you may be at a point in life where you still find it difficult to believe that the Lord wants to use you and bless you. You just can't *see* it.

I remember hearing about a terrible house fire that swept through the home of a young couple with four children. Mom and Dad got the little ones out safely, but one of their boys suddenly bolted back into the blazing house and dashed up the stairs to look for his pet. In just seconds flames turned that stairwell into a roaring inferno, and no one could run after him. Somehow the little boy found his way to an upstairs window, and the father yelled, "Son, jump! I can catch you! *Jump now!*"

Filled with terror, the boy wailed, "But, Daddy, I can't see you. I can't see you!"

His father immediately replied, "Son, it doesn't matter. I can see *you!*" Trusting his dad's voice, the little boy jumped blindly into the smoke...and into his father's arms.

Stalled in a dead end of hesitation and doubt, you may find yourself saying, "Lord, I can't see You. I'm in the middle of all this hurt and confusion, and I can't see Your hand in any of this. I can't see Your love and care in any of this. I can't see Your purpose in any of this. I want You to use me...but it's so dark!"

And that's where the Lord would say to us, too, "What matters is that I can see you, and I *do* know what I'm doing. You can jump into all My purposes for you, and I won't let you fall."

Whether you find yourself stepping out of a fiery window, out of a boat at sea, or out of your comfort zone in an abomination called Space Mountain, you'll find His arms strong enough to catch you and His grip firm enough to guide and comfort you wherever your path may lead.

[1] Andraé Crouch, "Through It All" (Valencia, Calif.: Manna Music, 1971).

Chapter Five

RUN HOME!

I f you've never seen a T-ball game, you don't know what you're missing.

If you've ever found yourself feeling cynical and fed up with those pampered pro athletes whining about their multimillion dollar contracts, take a little walk down to the neighborhood ball field some fine summer morning. Get a fresh taste for the pure joy of the game.

These T-ball guys are tiny. They're so small that half the numbers on their jerseys tuck into their pants. They can hardly hold a bat, let alone swing one. They're just discovering this thing called organized sports, and get wildly excited about it. They might not always do the right thing at the right time, but whatever they lack in skills they make up for with heart and huge enthusiasm.

I remember hearing about a little T-ball player named Bobby. It was his first T-ball game ever, and he was ready because his dad had taught him everything he needed to know. Well, almost.

Bobby walked up to the plate with a swagger that would make Ken Griffey Jr. jealous. And when he swung at the ball, he really let fly. One of his hits sailed into the outfield, sending the opposing team scrambling madly to retrieve it.

Bobby was excited. In fact, he got so excited he forgot to run.

"Bobby! RUN!" screamed his coach. The boy looked around, realized time was running out, and took off like a cottontail. In spite of the momentary lapse at home plate, this looked like a sure, in-the-park home run.

As Bobby rounded second, his coach cupped his hands over his mouth and yelled, "Now, run home as fast as you can! *Run home, Bobby!*"

Bobby ran home. After a slight hesitation, he made a sharp left, ran straight across the infield, over the pitcher's mound, and neatly slid home, totally bypassing third base.

The other team cheered. Bobby's team groaned. The coach was a study in disbelief. He stood frozen in position with his hand pressed into his forehead. Then, realizing that his player had taken him completely literally, he walked over to home plate to console the bewildered boy.

When coach said, "Run home," Bobby picked up his heels and ran home.

Truthfully, that works pretty well as a life strategy. There are times when you need to cut through all the complications, conditions, and complexities and just run straight home to the Lord as fast as your feet can carry you.

It's what John the Baptist did in possibly the most dis-couraging moments of his life.

DOUBTS IN THE DARK

John was a nonpaying guest in Herod's prison, and most likely he knew he would never leave it alive.

And he was troubled.

It wasn't because of the accommodations. He was used to sleeping on the ground with a rock for a pillow. It wasn't because of the food. When you've dined on locusts and honey for years on end, most anything will serve. And it really wasn't because his life was in jeopardy. It was just that if he had to face that executioner, he wanted to be *sure* about what he was doing, about why he was giving his life. In his heart, he wanted to make a strong recommitment to Jesus Christ. His whole life had been consumed with announcing this Messiah.

But now…he was troubled.

The longer he sat in his dreary cell, the more troubled he became. That's the way it is when you're in a dungeon. Looking around at those walls, it's a little tough to adjust your attitude. Finally John made a decision. What would it hurt if he asked a couple of his men to go to the Nazarene? What harm would there be in asking Him a couple of questions?

> *And when John had heard in prison about the works of Christ, he sent two of his disciples and said to Him, "Are You the Coming One, or do we look for another?"* (Matthew 11:2–3)

What do you do when you come to a time like that in your life, when discouragement has so flooded your soul that you wonder if you'll be able to go on? What do you do when you feel like you've come to the end, and begin to question things you've always been sure about?

John did exactly the right thing.

He ran home.

He went straight to the Lord.

He may have been confused. He may have been troubled. He may have been uncertain. He was certainly discouraged. But he was right on target with how he responded to that situation. In essence, he turned to the Lord and said, "I want to know. And there's no one else who can tell me. You're the Source."

He didn't run from the Lord and brood in silence. He didn't withdraw and reconsider his options. He took the initiative. He sent messengers to the Lord and asked for an immediate audience. By this action he was saying, "I believe You are the One. And it looks like I may be about to die for You. But I don't want to be foolish! I don't want to waste my life. If I'm going to die, I want it to be for the right reason. In my heart of hearts, I want to be sure."

What caused John's discouragement? The same thing that often causes you and me to feel the same way. John's *expectations* weren't being fulfilled. He had pictured events going in a certain direction at a certain time, and it wasn't turning out that way at all. What he had expected to be happening was not happening with this Messiah. He had carefully listened to all the accounts and all the rumors and all the eyewitness reports, and it just didn't seem to be adding up for him. This Jesus didn't seem to be putting the ax to the root of the tree, as John had prophesied. He was not overturning the corrupt religious establishment. His kingdom was not supplanting that of the evil Roman Empire.

John was puzzled. It wasn't making sense according to his logic. The Messianic train seemed to be moving away, down the wrong track, and he didn't feel on board anymore. And sitting there in prison, things kept looking worse and worse.

Like so many of us, John was facing a time of weakness and discouragement. But what he *did* with that discouragement was most important. Instead of letting it estrange him from Christ, he let it drive him into His presence. He admitted to the Lord that he felt confused. He told the Lord where he was struggling. *And in that groping and confusion, he determined to go right back to Jesus Christ for answers.*

And what did Jesus say about it after John's men had departed?

> *"What did you go out into the wilderness to see? A reed shaken by the wind? But what did you*

go out to see? A man clothed in soft garments?
Indeed, those who wear soft clothing are in
king's houses." (Matthew 11:7–8)

Reeds grew along the Jordan River by the multitudes. They bent and rustled, vacillating and bowing before every puff of wind. "So what kind of man did you come out to the wilderness to hear?" Jesus asked the crowds. "Just your everyday, garden variety sort of guy who shifts his convictions with the breeze or every ripple of public opinion? You needn't have bothered to come all the way out to the wilderness for that! You could have found those types in the king's palace or the temple!"

John was a man with a burning sense of mission and great self-control. He was a strong man, a man of convictions. His road would inevitably bring him into conflict with the authorities, and he was prepared to pay the price.

But when he was alone, in the dark, he came to a dead end where even strong men and women falter. Even the greats of the faith hit the wall of discouragement from time to time.

A FRIEND IN DISGUISE

Nearly every Monday or Tuesday of Charles Spurgeon's long ministry, he would receive a sharply critical letter.

And it was always from the same man.

You would think that after a while he would have disregarded those weekly missiles. But he always opened them, and they always caused him pain and frustration. They never failed to find their mark. The letters dripped with discouragement, and this self-appointed critic seemed to know just what words would sting and wound the pastor most.

This apparently went on for *years*, and later in life Spurgeon wrote about it in his diary. That one man, he reflected, had been one of the great reasons for his success in the ministry because every time he got that letter, it devastated him! But Spurgeon added (to paraphrase), "I'd always take it to the Lord. I would say, 'Lord, is he right? Lord, is this true? Am I really that bad? Do I preach that poorly? Am I not pastoring in the way that I should?' He kept me humble, but he also kept me looking to the Lord for strength to endure."

Spurgeon ran home.

He tucked those letters in his hip pocket and ran straight to his Lord Jesus. Where did he learn to do that? It's very possible that the great preacher learned that technique from one of his most beloved biblical heroes.

A DIAMOND DISPLAYED ON BLACK

A deeply emotional man, David knew all about the "high highs" and the "low lows." He, too, felt the wounds of unjust criticism. In one passage Scripture tells us just what David did in a low period of his life.

> *Now David was greatly distressed, for the people spoke of stoning him, because the soul of all the people was grieved, every man for his sons and his daughters. But David strengthened himself in the LORD his God.* (1 Samuel 30:6)

What happened next? The Bible tells us that David "inquired of the Lord." David immediately sought counsel from God Himself, and Scripture says, "He answered him" (1 Samuel 30:8).

An insightful note in *The Spirit-Filled Life Bible* says that although "grieving to the point of exhaustion, David uses the occasion to strengthen himself in the LORD his God, while the people, and very likely his soldiers, turn the energy of their grief to thoughts of assassination. Psalm 25 could have been composed at this time. It reflects David's trust in God at times of great danger and crisis."[1]

David was "greatly distressed." And no wonder! It wasn't

just critical letters or nasty little notes in the offering that had him worried. These people were talking about *stoning* him. In my years of ministry I'm sure I've had plenty of people angry and disgusted with me. But never quite that disgusted!

Yet out of this experience came a psalm.

A song grew up out of David's deep distress and discouragement. It came because David tucked his discouragement under one arm and ran to the Lord. He didn't want to see a counselor or a therapist or a support group. He wanted *God.*

David ran home.

And when he fell facedown in God's presence and poured out his heart…a little song began to stir inside him.

Do you want to see a beautiful, brilliant jewel lying on a backdrop blacker than a January midnight? Then spend a little time today in Psalm 25. Praise to the Lord, of course, is always beautiful. Songs of trust and hope in Him are always appropriate. But there is something unusually rare and lovely about an expression of faith when it rises out of a well of deep trouble and discouragement. It has a little extra luster to its beauty. It has a purer, sweeter sound to the listening ear.

That's what makes this psalm so wonderful. This was probably the lowest moment in the young man's life to this point. Think back to a couple of your own "lowest moments."

Recall your own dead ends of discouragement. Remember how you felt.

Now listen to a few of David's words, bubbling up from the depths of this dark pool…

To You, O LORD, I lift up my soul.

O my God, I trust in You;

Let me not be ashamed;

Let not my enemies triumph over me....

Show me Your ways, O LORD;

Teach me Your paths.

Lead me in Your truth and teach me,

For You are the God of my salvation;

On You I wait all the day....

My eyes are ever toward the LORD,

For He shall pluck my feet out of the net.

Turn Yourself to me, and have mercy on me,

For I am desolate and afflicted.

The troubles of my heart have enlarged;

Bring me out of my distresses!

Look on my affliction and my pain,

And forgive all my sins....

For I wait for You.

Psalm 25:1–2, 4–5, 15–18, 21

What was causing David's discouragement?

- He was discouraged by his enemies (vv. 2, 19–20). He was afraid they would shame him. He knew they hated him.

- He was discouraged by his own sins (vv. 7, 11, 18). He knew how great they were. He knew how certain habits had hounded him from his youth.

- He was discouraged by a feeling of confusion. He didn't know where to turn or which way to go. (vv. 4–5, 8–9).

- He was discouraged by his many troubles (vv. 16–18). His heart was so heavy. His pain was so constant. His distress never seemed to stop.

Tired of trying to sort it all out, untie all the knots, and make sense of everything, David just ran home as fast as he could. He "strengthened himself in the Lord his God." He drank deeply from the Artesian Well of encouragement.

HOW FAR ON ONE TANK?

Spiritual encouragement is a renewable resource. But like backpackers with canteens, you and I can carry just so much in our souls. Then we run dry. We must return again and again to the Lord, the never-failing Source of encouragement, to replenish our supply.

It *has* to be that way. If we never ran low, if we never found our little water bottles empty, we wouldn't keep coming back to Him. But we simply weren't built to carry around a two-hundred-gallon tank on our backs. It's more like a one- or two-gallon tank, and we go through it pretty fast — even on a normal day. And when it's gone, we're DIS-couraged. We're out of courage, and we need to come back to Him, get on our knees in His presence, and obtain a fresh supply.

God intended that we live our lives in this way so that we would turn to Him again and again in our need and in our emptiness. He wants a continual relationship with us. He wants us to walk *with* the Spirit.

When Scripture commands us to "be filled with the Spirit," as in Ephesians 5:18, a literal translation points toward a continuous, all-the-time filling of the Spirit. Be filled every hour! Be filled every day! Why?

Because this world is going to dry you up.

Everyday relationships are going to drain you.

The pressures of life are going to deplete you.

Struggles with Satan and the flesh are going to drag you down.

God says, "Be sure to come back to Me tomorrow. I'll fill you again so that you can carry on another day and give some more...love some more...lift some more...and serve some more in My name."

Satan also knows we can only go so far on one small "tank" of encouragement. The enemy knows that if he can keep us from turning to the Lord — as John the Baptist and David turned to Him — then he's got us!

It's strange, but most of us have a curious case of amnesia when it comes to obtaining encouragement. Deep down we know where to go. We know our Source. But the next time we're discouraged, the answer slips our minds somehow. We try to tough it out or dabble with other answers — shallow answers that can never truly satisfy us.

Where do you look when you are discouraged? I'll tell you what Ron Mehl does. When life closes in on me, and I'm in over my head and don't know what to do…I run home.

I close the door to my office, get down on my knees in front of the couch, and say, "Lord, it's me again. Here I am again. I want to make it, and I'm going to make it…but I thought You ought to know that I'm running a little low in the courage department. Would You help me, Lord?"

THE HELP BUTTON

For some reason, you and I tend toward the most complicated solutions to our problems, when a simple one will do. We tell ourselves, "It can't be that clear-cut. It can't be that simple. It's got to be more complicated than that."

I've never been mechanically — or electronically — inclined, to say the least. To any casual observer that must have been obvious a few weeks ago as I struggled to take a few baby steps on my new laptop computer. It may have been the hardware, it may have been the software, it may have been the Monday…but whatever it was, I just couldn't get where I needed to go. And it seemed like every button I pushed and every selection I made got me in that much deeper.

Where in the world am I, and how did I get here?

So I was pecking away at that thing, talking to myself and becoming more and more frustrated because I couldn't make it do what I needed it to do.

While I was sitting there, a little nine-year-old girl strolled into my office to greet me. Maybe someone had sent her in to cheer me up. Anyway, she walked over to where I was laboring and sat down beside me.

I looked down into that friendly little face and smiled.

"I don't think I know how to work this thing!" I told her.

She looked at me and said gravely, "You know, Pastor, when you work at a computer, you have to *think*."

I thought, *Thanks a lot, Sweetie. That's a big help.*

"Well," I said. "I think I'm in trouble."

Quick as a wink her little finger shot across my keyboard and pushed a button, a button I really hadn't paid any attention to.

It said, "Help."

And just that fast, the very instructions I needed jumped up onto the screen in three simple steps.

"Well — where did *that* come from?" I asked.

She smiled back at me tolerantly.

"You know," I told her, "I think I'm going to keep you around for a while so that whenever I get into trouble you can just sit here with me and help me work this."

Truthfully, my young visitor was wiser than I was. She knew how to push the help button, and that was a summons even the stubborn electronic brain couldn't ignore. I might have struggled with submenus and operating systems and procedures for hours — finally giving it all up as useless and wasted time.

But my little friend knew just what to do — in an instant.

The Lord knows all about us. He knows how we get tangled up in the complexities of life. He knows that we tend to bang around with pots and pans and elaborate recipes in the kitchen with Martha, rather than sitting quietly at His feet like Mary.

That's why He gives us in our Bibles so many good

examples of what to do. That's why He sends little girls in pink tennis shoes into our offices to push the help button on our computers.

Life really isn't as difficult and complicated as we make it out to be sometimes.

Forget about crossing all those t's and dotting all those i's and touching all the bases.

Just run home.

[1] *Spirit-Filled Life Bible* (Nashville: Thomas Nelson, Inc., 1991), 436.

Chapter Six

THE
GREAT
INTRUDER

Every job has its moments.

Sure, there are tedious times. And frustrating times. And times when you're just plain working your tail off and can't wait for the end of your day or the end of your shift. It's part of what "work" means on a fallen planet. God told Adam that by the sweat of his brow he would earn his bread, and most every son of Adam and daughter of Eve since that time have understood something about sweaty brows, sore backs, tired muscles, and weary minds.

Still…every job has its moments. Its golden interludes. Its little pinnacles of fulfillment. Even if only a few.

Even Adam must have looked up from his newly invented hoe every now and then, straightened his back, mopped his brow, watched Eve hanging out the laundry, and little Seth laughing and throwing dirt clods at the crows. And then he must have looked around at the beauty of his still-new world and found reason to thank God for life.

A pastor's job has its golden moments, too. Actually, a great many of them. And for me, weddings rate right up there at the top. There's nothing like them. They can be sad and happy and solemn and hilarious all at the same time. Yet one particular wedding lingers in my memory for reasons very different than the usual.

This day would be an utter delight. From the time we unlocked the church door on that Saturday morning in August, emotion rippled through the air like a playful breeze. It was a double wedding and was especially meaningful because the brides' father, Bill Estep, had been stricken with a serious brain tumor and was given only months to live. Bill and JoAnn are dear to me, so being a part of this wedding meant the world. Tim Hval was marrying Joelle Estep, and Jon Carmichael was marrying Brittni Estep. Everyone sensed God's smile and walked a tightrope between laughter and happy tears all morning — with plenty of both to go around.

At half past one, right on schedule, I completed the ceremony and raised my hands to pray and dismiss the guests to the reception. When I finished praying, the full house in our worship center spontaneously stood up and applauded!

I was surprised and pleased. That doesn't happen very often at weddings. I walked down the steps of the platform and started up the sloping center aisle, surrounded by wide smiles, happy chatter, and ladies dabbing their eyes with handkerchiefs.

At that very moment I felt something strange in my chest.

Tim and Joelle were waiting for me upstairs. I was supposed to sign the marriage certificate before they went over to the reception. But by the time I got to the top of the stairs, a wave of clammy coldness had swept through me, and a pain like I've never felt before or since began to tear into my chest. There they were, bride and groom, flushed and happy, waiting for me to sign the certificate. It was all so normal and routine and right. I'd done it hundreds of times. Yet at that moment nothing seemed normal, routine, or right. I was suddenly swimming in a sea of intense pain, desperately trying to keep my head above water.

"Here," I said, forcing a smile and trying to sound normal, "would you kids begin to sign on these lines? I'll — be right back."

But as I ducked out of the room and walked ever so carefully back down those stairs, I knew I wouldn't be coming back for a very long time.

If at all.

That's the way it is with the dead end of serious illness or injury.

There's a sense of unreality about it. How could something so foreign, so intrusive, so alien and strange suddenly burst into "normal" life and make such massive changes? It seems like you ought to be able to shake it off, like a bad dream that lingers as you sit on the edge of your bed. It seems like you ought to be able to hang up on it, like an irritating telephone solicitor who's just interrupted your favorite supper. *I don't WANT this call right now!* It seems like you ought to be able to put it out of your mind and go back to work or back to school or back to bed or back to life as you've always known it.

But you can't. It doesn't go away. It elbows in, gets in your face, and intrudes to the point that you can't even pretend normality any longer. Your winding street or broad avenue has come to a dead end and — whether you like it or not, whether you acknowledge it or not — the course of your life's journey is abruptly changed.

It must have been that way for Naaman, too.

CHARIOT ON A DEAD END

At first it was probably nothing more than a curious little patch on his neck. A sore that wouldn't heal. It was ridiculous — absurd — that something so small should suddenly signal a terrible end to such a grand and marvelous career. And yet that's just what it did.

Here's how Scripture begins Naaman's fascinating story:

> *Now Naaman, commander of the army of the*
> *king of Syria, was a great and honorable man*

in the eyes of his master, because by him the
LORD had given victory to Syria. He was also a
mighty man of valor, but a leper. (2 Kings 5:1)

Did you notice that little, three-letter word "but"? Before that word, everything was glorious and positive.

This man Naaman commanded the army of one of the world's great powers. A great and mighty man. A valued and valorous soldier. An honored and trusted counselor to his king. A leader touched by the Lord, who had known victory on every side.

But…

BUT…

He was a leper.

And with that one small qualifier, the whole picture changed. Everything in life became defined and confined by those last three words: "but a leper." Today it would be akin to describing a man's impressive titles, dazzling accomplishments, and outstanding honors, and then ending the description by adding, "but he has AIDS." What would you remember about that introduction? Suddenly all the noteworthy and marvelous parts of that description go out the window, and you're left with the dread. The gloom. The stigma.

Naaman was a powerful man and a highly decorated war

hero. I can imagine him driving a huge, formidable chariot drawn by prancing stallions — Syria's finest. But he was headed for an unthinkably horrible dead end. He knew it. And there wasn't a thing in the world to be done about it.

Or so he thought.

> *And the Syrians had gone out on raids, and had brought back captive a young girl from the land of Israel. She waited on Naaman's wife. Then she said to her mistress, "If only my master were with the prophet who is in Samaria! For he would heal him of his leprosy." And Naaman went in and told his master, saying, "Thus and thus said the girl who is from the land of Israel."* (vv. 2–4)

If illness or injury drops suddenly out of the blue heavens into our unsuspecting lives, changing and rearranging every-thing...*so does the grace of God.* The Lord of time and eternity is neither surprised nor shaken by the events that crash into these fragile, time-bound lives of ours. But He does care very much. Hebrews 4:15 tells us that He is "touched with the feeling of our infirmities" (KJV).

The trouble is, we may not always recognize that grace when it arrives!

We're so upset or troubled or shaken by our circumstances that, if we're not careful, we may miss the small, gentle methods He uses to speak grace and healing into our lives. Even Paul missed it, when he struggled with a distressing, lingering illness. He wanted instant healing, but the Lord said to him, "Paul, My grace is enough for you! You may not receive everything you want right now, but you will receive more of Me! I *will* touch your life with My grace." (See 2 Corinthians 12:7–10.)

In the case of Naaman (the great and mighty), the voice of hope and healing came through the sigh of a foreign slave girl (the meek and lowly). Mrs. Naaman, to her everlasting credit, heeded the little girl's words and related them to her husband. And her husband took them to the king of Syria.

Eventually the distinguished general arrived at the prophet Elisha's humble door in Samaria. You can safely bet that no one in Elisha's neighborhood had ever seen a mightier man in a more awesome war chariot. Kids and dogs, merchants and housewives began to edge closer for a better look. Gold accents glinted in the sunlight. The powerful war horses blew and stamped and nodded their regal heads.

> *And Elisha sent a messenger to him, saying, "Go and wash in the Jordan seven times, and your flesh shall be restored to you, and you shall be clean." (2 Kings 5:10)*

You probably could have heard a collective gasp go up from the crowd. Elisha wasn't even coming out of the house to meet this man in person? And he had the nerve to tell this Great One to go *where* and to do *what?*

> *But Naaman became furious, and went away*
> *and said, "Indeed, I said to myself, 'He will*
> *surely come out to me, and stand and call on*
> *the name of the LORD his God, and wave his*
> *hand over the place, and heal the leprosy.'*
> *Are not the Abanah and the Pharpar, the rivers*
> *of Damascus, better than all the waters of*
> *Israel? Could I not wash in them and be clean?"*
> *So he turned and went away in a rage.*
> (vv. 11–12)

Naaman had a lot to learn about this God of Israel. His thoughts were not Naaman's thoughts. His ways were not Naaman's ways. But within those thoughts of the Lord was Naaman's healing. And within those ways of the Lord was life — even eternal life. But the *response* was up to Naaman. He could "preserve his dignity" and thunder back to Syria in a royal rage. He could sit in the dark in some isolated apartment outside of Damascus and watch his flesh crumble away. Or, he could humble himself greatly and accept the Lord's salvation.

And his servants came near and spoke to him,
and said, "My father, if the prophet had told
you to do something great, would you not have
done it? How much more then, when he says to
you, 'Wash, and be clean'?" So he went down
and dipped seven times in the Jordan, according
to the saying of the man of God; and his flesh
was restored like the flesh of a little child, and
he was clean. (vv. 13–14)

Naaman's life and career had been seriously disrupted by his disease. But on the seventh humiliating dip in the Jordan, he came up out of that water a changed man — in more ways than one.

Then he returned to the man of God, he and all
his aides, and came and stood before him; and he
said, "Indeed, now I know that there is no God
in all the earth, except in Israel.... Your servant
will no longer offer either burnt offering or sacri-
fice to other gods, but to the LORD." (vv. 15, 17)

Naaman had come to a dead end, a dead end he had despised and resisted with everything in him. And yet in that place of hurt and humbling and sorrow, he found greater treasure than in all the palaces of Syria. He had been compelled to bow very low. And yet when he stood up again, he saw that the way before him was clear...and brighter than he could have ever believed.

A WAY PREPARED

Those thoughts might very well have comforted me as I staggered down the stairs that Saturday morning in August. But when you're scared and in terrible pain, you can hardly think of anything beyond bare survival.

I came to the bottom of the steps, walked about ten feet, and saw Debbie, who works in my office.

"Debbie," I said, "would you take me to the hospital?"

Her eyes got very wide, and she turned around and hurried toward the car. I walked out the door to the parking lot — something I probably shouldn't have done — and got in the passenger side. Debbie began driving. The pain was unbelievably intense — now shooting through both of my arms and hands. I couldn't have conceived that pain like that was possible.

"Debbie, Debbie," I said, "please go through this stoplight. Don't stop, Debbie, don't stop."

Now Debbie is a good driver, but she's never going to be a threat at Daytona. What I needed right then was a little less caution and a lot more speed. And for my sake, bless her heart, she did it. She stepped on the accelerator and — rather sheepishly — ran every red light on the five-minute trip to St. Vincent's Hospital. Even so, it was the longest five minutes of my whole life.

We pulled into the emergency circle, and by then I knew I wouldn't be able to walk — or even move. Sweat had soaked all the way through my shirt and my suit. I was wringing wet with it.

At the very moment we pulled up to the double glass doors of the emergency entrance, an ambulance attendant was coming out the doors, pushing an empty wheelchair back to his ambulance. He saw us and immediately wheeled the chair over to my door.

Almost as though we were expected.

He opened my door and said, "Sir, do you need help?"

"Yeah — I think so."

He helped me out of my coat and into the wheelchair and wheeled me through the doors. The ER personnel immediately laid me down on a bed and wired me to an EKG unit.

As they were running through a rapid series of tests, I remember a young intern leaning over me and saying, "Dr. Mehl, you're having a heart attack."

I just looked at him, but I felt like saying, "And you went

to school for fifteen years to tell me *that?* I could have told you that when I drove up!"

Several physicians were standing in the hallway outside the emergency room, chatting with each other, when they wheeled me in. One of the doctors who saw me come through the door "happened" to be the father of a new laser heart surgery — still in development.

He walked over to where I was lying, glanced at my vital signs, and said, "Dr. Mehl, we're working on a new procedure. A new kind of surgery — with a laser. If you're willing, we would like your permission to perform this procedure. Now."

"Sure," I said. "Let's go for it."

"Okay," he replied, "we need to go. Right away. Let's *move.*"

And move we did. After that, everything began happening very fast...and it blurs in my memory. Crushing pain and pressure. A speeding gurney. Lights on the ceiling. An elevator. Faces. Voices. Needles.

I would later learn that I had suffered a very serious heart attack, with total blockage in one of my heart's arteries. In essence, I was dying from the first moment I felt the pain. A portion of my heart was getting no blood at all, and how long can a heart go on beating without blood?

But by God's grace, I did live. And recovered. With a few

exceptions, I'm back on my old schedule, doing everything I did before. And as I've reflected on that momentous Saturday, I've been amazed at the evidences of God's kindness and grace.

- He let me finish the wedding.
- Debbie was standing at the bottom of the stairs.
- The car was nearby.
- An ambulance driver met me with a wheelchair.
- A renowned team of heart surgeons perfecting a quick new technique were literally standing around in the hallway outside the emergency room — on a Saturday afternoon!
- My recovery was surprisingly rapid.
- God has allowed me to continue my ministry and been pleased to bless it.

Some might waste time and emotional energy wrestling with the question, "Why did this have to happen to me?" But I choose to see and remember those wonderful points of God's grace toward me all along the way. God had already prepared my way for arrival at that dead end. He had gone before me, well in advance, to get things ready and set everything in order.

But what, you might ask, if I had died in that emergency room? (A strong possibility) What then?

Ultimately, nothing would have been much different. His

timing still would have been perfect. I still would have had an escort: Instead of an ambulance attendant with a wheelchair, it would have been an angel in a chariot. I still would know that He had gone before me, well in advance, preparing for my arrival. Instead of a renowned heart surgeon speaking in my ear, it would have been the One who formed my heart and made me for Himself. Instead of an intern telling me, "Dr. Mehl, you're having a heart attack," it would have been my Lord Jesus Himself, saying, "Welcome home, My brother. Everything is ready for you."

From the smallest, most insignificant of dead ends, through a serious heart attack, and even to death itself, this is the God who goes before us. This is the God who meets us at every dead end with His provision and His presence.

But why did He allow that terrible heart attack? Why does God permit these crushing physical setbacks to intrude into our lives? Is it all a waste?

THE GIFT OF PERSPECTIVE

Not only did I learn that He had arranged things through my crisis, but I learned that I needed to be arranging things, too. On the first Sunday I was allowed to preach after my recuperation, I spoke from Psalm 90:12:

So teach us to number our days,
That we may gain a heart of wisdom.

To "number" means to evaluate, consider, or take inventory. In the busyness of life and the press of responsibilities, it had been a long time since I'd slowed down enough to reflect on my life and ministry. Was I pouring my life's energies in the best directions? If I had died in that car on the way to the hospital, were there areas of my life I would have been ashamed about as I stood before my Lord?

As I rested and healed, I took inventory. I considered. I waited on Him for perspective and wisdom. I sought His counsel and confirmation on the ways I had been expending myself. And I determined in my heart to please Him with however many days He chose to give me in this life. Through it all, I became aware that He was doing a deeper work in my life. I might understand a little of that, but I may not grasp very much of it this side of heaven.

A DEEPER WORK

Paul, no stranger to suffering, and a man who had looked death in the face on more than one occasion, offers these amazing observations:

For all things are for your sakes, that grace, hav-
ing spread through the many, may cause thanks-
giving to abound to the glory of God. Therefore
we do not lose heart. Even though our outward
man is perishing, yet the inward man is being
renewed day by day. For our light affliction,
which is but for a moment, is working for us a
far more exceeding and eternal weight of glory,
while we do not look at the things which are
seen, but at the things which are not seen. For
the things which are seen are *temporary, but the*
things which are not seen are eternal.

(2 Corinthians 4:15–18)

When it comes right down to it, you and I don't see very
much or very far. Our eyes skim the surface of things. We
notice those temporary landmarks near at hand, and yet each
one of us is being swept rapidly along toward the great sea of
eternity, which we can't see at all. Serious illness or injury
forces us to take a longer view, to reconsider what is truly
important.

Naaman had thought politics and battles and chariot races
and royal pomp and splendor were the most important things
of life. But in his suffering he learned that those things didn't
count for much at all. Coming up out of the muddy waters of

the humble Jordan, he had come face to face with his Creator — and learned the true purpose for life.

In the passage just cited, Paul called his troubles "light" and "momentary," when they must have felt crushingly heavy and unending at times. There were times when the pressure on his life seemed so great that he despaired of life itself (see 2 Corinthians 1:8–11). In what sense, then, were they "light" and "momentary"? They were light in comparison with what he knew Christ had suffered and endured on the cross. *And they were momentary when he compared them with eternity.* Paul knew that his entrance into that eternity was just a few short years away.

As I've struggled with ongoing leukemia for more than ten years, at times it feels like I've had it for a century. And yet these ten years are the merest blip — a flicker of light you see out of the corner of your eye — when compared to the endless, shining ages of eternity so near at hand.

Paul says that God "is working for us a far more exceeding and eternal weight of glory." Through your physical setbacks, He is doing a deeper work in your life. He is bringing "weight" to your life that couldn't come any other way or by any other avenue.

How distressing and discouraging life becomes when we lose this eternal perspective! It's as though we're trying to live on a flat piece of paper, in a two-dimensional world with no depth of meaning or anticipation or joy. We cannot "read" the Christian life on the basis of individual circumstances. We must not place our focus on individual events such as a heart attack, an illness, or an injury. If we do, we'll lose sight of the fact that there's a wider, deeper picture here. And it's an eternal one. It is a work that God is doing from beginning to end.

Only when you have acknowledged this deeper perspective can you say, "This is a light affliction. This is a temporary affliction. And as I trust Him, it is producing implications in my life that stretch right on into eternity."

In a verse I love very much, the psalmist writes:

> *My flesh and my heart fail;*
> *But God is the strength of my heart and my*
> *portion forever.*
>
> Psalm 73:26

Yes, this flesh of mine is failing. My health (and yours, too!) is unbelievably fragile. I've struggled with cancer. My heart muscle has been damaged. But where is my focus? On God, the Source of my strength. On God, who holds my life in His very hands, both now and forever. He is faithful!

When long-term pastor Doyle Masters was stricken with cancer, he penned these words to his beloved congregation:

The options open to me medically are minimal and at best do not promise renewed energy nor longevity. The other option is to turn this over to God in faith for His healing and ultimate will. What the future holds we do not know, but we do know that God holds it. These past few days have rolled over us like an avalanche, leaving in their wake some central certainties which make up my thanksgiving list. My thanksgiving list is made this year, not from what I have, but from who has me. A God who is able to do exceedingly above all that I ask or think.

That's really the message at this dead end, isn't it?

You and I have that tendency in our flesh to continually place our confidence and hope in the wrong things — in things which can be shaken rather than that which cannot be shaken. Pastor Masters spoke of the certainties that remain after the avalanche. And health just isn't certain. It *never* is. All of us live on a hair's breadth. When you think about it, we're only here until our next heartbeat, our next brain wave, our next breath.

Certainty in this life has nothing to do with good fortune or good health. But it has everything to do with the goodness, faithfulness, and steadfast love of God.

Chapter Seven

A MAN
WITH
NO HANDS

Y
ou've never truly experienced downtown Portland, Oregon, until you've been there on a cold, rainy day.

Forget all that nonsense about sunshine and rose gardens and postcard views of Mount Hood. The definitive Portland experience occurs on a slate gray afternoon in a twenty-mile-an-hour wind when you park too far from where you want to go, feel cold rain seeping down your back collar, and step into a curbside puddle that surges over the top of your loafers.

When *that* happens, you can say, "I, too, have experienced Portland."

Portland sidewalks, of course, were never intended for browsing, window-shopping, or amiable strolling. They're only wet runways meant to launch Portlanders from Point A to Point B — Point B usually being an espresso shop or a bookstore. No one really looks at each other on the streets of Portland because everyone is either cocooned in the shelter of an umbrella or striding miserably along with chin buried somewhere near the breastbone.

Joyce and I were hurrying through the rain with the rest of Portland and were about to duck into the congenial shelter of a Nordstrom's, when I saw the man with no hands.

He was selling tiny American flags and clutched one in the

merest stub of a little finger. We paused at the entrance of the store, then walked over to where he was standing. The wind was driving the rain at a malicious angle. Somehow it seemed to be flying up under my topcoat and pants legs, chilling me to the bone. Yet something made us want to spend a moment or two with the little man standing out in the rain.

He was short, with a weathered, unshaven face, and the most tired looking eyes I've ever seen outside of a hospital. He could have been in his late thirties or his late fifties — it was impossible to tell. His tattered fatigue jacket was soaked with rain, his surplus combat boots down at the heels.

We talked for a while. Reaching out with his stub of a finger, he handed me one of his tiny flags, and I thanked him. Joyce nudged me, reminding me I was supposed to give him some money in exchange for the flag, which I did.

I got up the nerve to ask, "What happened to your hands?" (After giving him a little money, I guess I thought I had the right to ask.)

He looked at me with those tired, faraway eyes, rain streaming down his face, and said, "Well, I was workin' on a farm. Got my right hand caught in a hay baler. When it got caught, my first reaction was to try to pull it out, see? I reached in with my other hand and — it gobbled up that one, too. It cut both my hands off, 'cept for this little bit of finger."

"How long ago did this happen?"

"Fifteen years."

Fifteen years. I thought I could see the weight of those years, settled on his shoulders and in the lines of his face.

"I don't have nothin'," he told me in a matter-of-fact tone. "I really can't do nothin'. Obviously I'm a drunk. You can see that. You know that. It's no shock to you."

We conversed a while longer, then I reached into my pocket, took out all the money I had, and gave it to him. I tried to encourage him a little and talked to him about the Lord.

Then as we walked away into the rain, I felt vaguely stressed.

What's this all about, Lord? I found myself wondering. *Why did our paths cross today? What is it You want me to see here?*

At the time I didn't draw any special meaning or significance from this encounter. It was enough just to show the man a little compassion in the Lord's name and for the Lord's sake. As time has gone by, however, it seems as if the Holy Spirit has wanted me to hold this moment in my mental catalog of visual images...*a tired, used-up little man with no hands standing on a rainy street corner.*

Over the years I've come to understand that the man's name is Ron Mehl.

Yes, I've accomplished some things in my life and can do

a few things moderately well. And yes, I have two good hands, a family that loves me, a wonderful church, and a challenging ministry.

But I am *nothing* without Him.

After all these years of walking with Him, you'd think I would understand that pretty well by now, but it's something I've had to relearn ten thousand times: the futility — the utter emptiness and futility — of trying to accomplish something of eternal value in my own strength and in my own wisdom. It can't be done. For all the good I can do for Christ's kingdom in my own flesh, I might as well be standing on some street corner with no hands, hawking paper flags.

Even if I *want* to be a godly husband (and I do)…without His enabling, I can't do it.

Even if I *want* to be a God-pleasing father (I do — with all my heart)…without His help, it just won't happen.

Even if I *want* to be a Christlike pastor and shepherd (and the Lord knows my desire here)…without His working through me, this man can't get it done.

LEARNING THE SECRET EARLY

A young man came to see me in my office not long ago. He had recently come to know the Lord, and I knew it was the "real thing" because of his deep, brand-new desire to please God and to become a better husband and dad. What he wanted to know from me was where to start.

"What do I do, Pastor?" he asked. "What can I read? How can I learn more?"

"Well," I said, "I'll tell you just what my mom always told me."

"Okay." He seemed poised to hear something profound roll out of my mouth.

"Read your Bible."

"Yes…?"

"That's it. Open up your Bible and read what it says about being a husband. Read what it says about being a father. Read all the verses you can find about raising children. Read what it says about loving and serving and being an example. Just read your Bible and ask the Lord to speak to you."

"Oh," he said, looking a bit deflated. "Well. Thank you, Pastor." I don't know if that's what he'd been expecting when he came to see me, but that's what he got. I did take time to show him how to get into the Scriptures and find passages on all those subjects.

Some time later he came back to me, Bible in hand.

"Excuse me, Pastor," he said, "but — this is ridiculous!"

"What's ridiculous?"

"What it says in here!" he said, thumping his Bible. "Who can live like this? I mean…there's no way." He shook his head. "Just listen to some of this stuff, Pastor!" He read me several verses to prove just how ridiculous it really was.

> *Husbands, love your wives, just as Christ also loved the church and gave Himself for her.* (Ephesians 5:25)
>
> *Fathers, do not provoke your children to wrath, but bring them up in the training and admonition of the Lord.* (Ephesians 6:4)
>
> *Love suffers long and is kind; love does not envy.… [Love] bears all things, believes all things, hopes all things, endures all things. Love never fails.*
> (1 Corinthians 13:4, 7–8)

"Then how about *this* one," he went on. "This is really choice."

> *Be completely humble and gentle; be patient, bearing with one another in love.* (Ephesians 4:2, NIV)

"Who can live that way?" he demanded. "I mean — this is overwhelming. I'm sorry, Pastor," (and he looked truly grieved here) "but this just isn't me. I know me, and I don't have it in me to be like this."

It was quiet for a moment. Then I said, "You know what? You're really amazing."

"How? Why? What do you mean?"

"How long have you known the Lord? Just a few weeks now? Yet in those few weeks you've picked up on the whole secret of Christianity. Do you realize it took me *eleven years* to get where you are right now!"

I could see that I'd lost him, so I tried to explain. It's not possible to live the life of God…without the life of God. You can never be the person He wants you to be…until you *realize* you can never be the person He wants you to be. That's not double-talk; that's just simple reality. Only the Holy Spirit living in us can reproduce the life of Christ through us. It simply cannot be done any other way — no matter if you're Billy Graham, Pat Robertson, Mother Teresa, or the Pope. When Jesus told His men, "Without Me, you can do nothing" (John 15:5), He was stating the most basic, essential truth of the Christian life.

Now what does this really mean in a practical way? Obviously there are a great many people across our world who have no time for Jesus Christ and yet accomplish many amazing and wonderful things. When Jesus said, "Without Me you can do nothing," does that mean I can't get a job? No, I can get a job. Does that mean I can't marry a wife and have a family? No, I can get married and have a family. Does that mean I can't buy a house? No, I can buy a house. Does that mean I can't put together a budget or write a novel or design a sky-scraper or win the Nobel prize for physics? No, I could accomplish any or all of those things if I had the opportunities and training and natural ability.

You can do a lot of things without the Lord, but there's one thing you can't do: *You can't be like Him.*

You can sail a dinghy across the Pacific, you can complete the Boston Marathon in a wheelchair, you can sit on the Supreme Court and wrestle with great constitutional questions, you can write a piece of music that will make grown men weep, and you can create a two-story, stained-glass window that people from all over the world will come to applaud and admire. But you can't be what God wants you to be, and you can't do what God wants you to do without the specific, daily empowering of His Spirit. You can't bear spiritual fruit — not so much as a spiritual crabapple — unless the life of Christ is flowing in you and through you.

That's what I longed for my young friend to discover as he cracked the pages of his shiny new Bible. Try as he might, he could never find the power to be the kind of man he now longed to be without supernatural current surging through his wires.

I've come to believe that's why God brings us to those dead ends where we feel our personal inadequacy so keenly —

and so painfully. We say, "I'm in over my head! I can't do this! I could never do this!" And then, if we sit at that dead end long enough, we may remember (once again) that this is really nothing new. Because the truth is, we can't accomplish *anything* for Christ and His kingdom unless He does it in us and through us. It's as basic a lesson as you'll ever encounter, and you've probably heard it many times before. But most of us will wrestle and wrestle and WRESTLE with this fact of spiritual life as long as there's blood in our veins and breath in our lungs.

Just think what Moses had to go through.

A FORTY-YEAR DEAD END

In Moses' youth and strength and vigor, he desperately wanted the job of delivering Israel from her slavery to Egypt. He was the man to do it! He could feel it simmering in his marrow. Really, no one was better equipped to pull off the job. Moses was in his sinewy masculine prime and had the education, the opportunity, the power, the military training, and very possibly the personality and drive to make a viable run at it.

The net result, of course, was disaster.

No one wanted to follow him, the Egyptians tried to kill him, and he had to flee for his life into the backside of the wilderness without freeing a single soul.

Forty years later, when he was eighty, and after an entire career of desert sheepherding, Moses received a divine commission to deliver his nation. It was almost laughable. It was like one of the stories you hear about a guy's draft notice getting lost in the mail and being delivered half a century later to a retirement home. Absurd! Moses, that eccentric old sheepherder, deliver a nation? Any inclination he might have had in those directions had long since blown away on the wind. He had forgotten his education and training and had become a meek recluse, utterly lacking in self-confidence.

In their celebrated encounter at the burning bush, God had to pointedly tell His servant, in so many words, "Really, Moses, you don't need to worry about this job I'm laying before you. I know it's vast and great, but so am I! Frankly, you don't bring all that much to the party, anyway. You're concerned and worried about how you're going to accomplish such a daunting task and get all this done. But there isn't much you can offer that will make any difference one way or another! Just obey Me, follow My instructions, and *I'll* get it done — through you!"

> *And God said to Moses, "I AM WHO I AM."*
> *And He said, "Thus you shall say to the children of*
> *Israel, 'I AM has sent me to you.'"* (Exodus 3:14)

MEETING GOD AT A DEAD END

When God told Moses His name, "I AM WHO I AM," He was saying, "I'm everything that you're not! I'm capable of doing everything that needs to be done. I AM! Whatever you need, I'll supply."

Throughout the pages of the Bible, Old Testament and New, He demonstrates this again and again. And when does the lesson occur? It's almost always after His people have run smack into a brick wall and don't know where to turn or what to do.

Think of Philip, sitting on the hillside with Jesus, watching thousands upon thousands of people streaming up the mountain to see the Lord and hear Him teach.

> *Then Jesus lifted up His eyes, and seeing a*
> *great multitude coming toward Him, He said*
> *to Philip, "Where shall we buy bread, that these*
> *may eat?" But this He said to test him, for*
> *He Himself knew what He would do.*
> (John 6:5–6)

The question pushed poor Philip right into a dead end. He didn't have any idea what to say or what to do! Was the Lord seriously asking him for some kind of answer? Thinking that a quick crowd estimate might do the job, Philip whipped out his calculator and tried to crunch a few numbers.

Philip answered Him, "Two hundred denarii
worth of bread is not sufficient for them, that
every one of them may have a little."... Then
Jesus said, "Make the people sit down." (vv. 7, 10)

If Philip had only known it, he had just met God at a dead end. He was sitting within scant inches of the Creator of the universe. What are a few thousand loaves of bread to the One who holds all the rippling, golden wheat fields of the whole world in the palm of His hand? Philip was about to witness what this God could do.

And that's the way it is for us. When we come to the dead end of personal inadequacies, when we come to the dead end of depleted resources, He's right there. Not just inches away, but *inside* us! Closer than hands or feet, closer than breathing. And He will be to us all that He is.

SEVEN CENTS SHORT

Joyce lets me go to the grocery store about once every three years.

On one occasion not too long ago, she wasn't feeling very well, and I convinced her that she could rest easy this time and that I would handle the job. So off I went to our local Safeway, confident that I could remember the three or four items we needed without burdening myself with a written list.

But grocery stores are incredibly distracting. Going by the meat counter, I remembered how my mom used to fix chicken back home in Bloomington, Minnesota. Going down the snacks aisle, I remembered past football games and all the great junk food my boys and I had consumed. Wheeling down the cold cereal aisle, I noticed the absence of Sugar Jets, a childhood favorite of mine. It probably went out of fashion when the experts decided that sugar was bad for everyone in general and kids in particular. Walking past the dairy section, I remembered what I had said in a sermon from 1 Peter a few weeks before about desiring "the pure milk of the Word."

By the time I'd wandered up and down a few more memory lanes, my head was filled with competing images of my mom, Minnesota, stewed chicken, Super Sunday, Sugar Jets, and the Apostle Peter. But I didn't have a clue why I'd come to the store or what I was supposed to buy. Rather than admit defeat and call Joyce on a pay phone, I bought what I thought we *might* need — and some other stuff we'd never had before but that looked pretty good. Then I wheeled the cart up to the checkout counter.

Shooting the gaps like a pro, I maneuvered my cart straight into the line with the fewest people. *Well,* I thought, *that was rather well done.* Really the only one ahead of me was a little boy. He must have been about five. A little guy, and cute as could be. He was just tall enough — by standing on his toes — to get his chin on the counter. Both of his hands were on the counter, too, and in each hand he clutched one of those big, plastic-wrapped chunks of milk chocolate that come out of the bulk bins. One of the chunks was already starting to melt, so I could tell he'd held them for a while. He was gripping those things like there was no tomorrow.

I noticed that his coins were spread out on the counter and that the lady had just finished ringing up his purchase. She counted his coins, then looked down at him over the top of her glasses.

"Well, Honey," she said, "you're seven cents short."

I watched the tiny guy and couldn't help but love him. He's the type of little boy you'd like to scoop up in your pocket and take home. But now he was staring at this clerk, not sure what he was supposed to do.

"Oh," was all he could say, and he kept right on looking at her.

The clerk tried again. "I'm sorry, Honey, but you see, you won't be able to get the candy. This isn't enough. You don't have enough money. You'll have to take the candy back."

Wouldn't you know it, he started to cry. Two little tears ran down his upturned face. I was standing there feeling just sick about it. I kept thinking about my own two sons and how they might have felt in a moment like that.

After about ten seconds or so (it seemed like five minutes), he noticed me in his peripheral vision. His little head turned to look up at me. I'm about six-four, so he did have to look *up*. There I was, looking down at this grubby, tear-stained face. He didn't say a word, but his expression was eloquent.

How about it, Mister?

Now you might think I said, "And what do you want from *me?*" But I didn't say that. Looking down into that little face, I wanted to give him everything in my wallet. I reached into my pocket and handed the lady a dime. And the little boy — who had never let go of that candy for a moment — simply turned and left with the goods without a word or a thank-you.

As I drove home, I saw myself in that little boy. I saw Ron Mehl in that face peeking over the grocery counter. Seven cents short of a dime. Never having quite enough. In every dimension of my life...not quite enough. I could remember so many times feeling that sick sense of dread as Sunday drew near. Waking up to the realization that I had to preach again, and that I just didn't have it. Knowing that hundreds of people would be sitting there in that auditorium with upturned faces and expectant hearts — each of them needing a word from

God — and knowing that it wasn't in me! I didn't have it, and it was ridiculous to think I ever would.

With Moses, I would find myself saying, "Lord, who am I to proclaim your salvation?" With Philip I would find myself crying out, "Lord, how can I possibly feed all those hungry people? It's crazy! Even if they all got only one bite, I wouldn't have enough! I'm not just seven cents short, I'm a million dollars short!"

And I would find myself looking up at God, like a kid at the grocery counter who's under pressure and out of pennies. God always has something to spare...whether it's a dime, a Snickers bar, a few thousand loaves of bread, the ability to speak forth His word in season, or just two strong hands when I feel especially weak and short handed.

This is a God who knows all about our inadequacies and shortfalls. And there's nothing He loves better than when His kids look to Him to make up the difference.

Chapter Eight

WAKING UP ON A DEAD END

The Apostle Peter had the spiritual gift of falling asleep.

No matter what the situation, no matter what trouble and mayhem raged around him, the big fisherman could slip into a semicoma and neatly detach himself from the woes and anxieties of the world.

Really, of course, it was no gift at all. It ended up costing Peter very, very dearly.

Peter's ongoing struggle with his eyelids reminds me of a young associate pastor I know. I've always liked this guy, and I was happy to hear he'd landed a staff position at a good-sized church. Really, he has a lot going for him. Multigifted. Knows the Word. Loves the Lord. But...he has this little problem with falling asleep.

In his first few weeks at the new church, he was extra concerned about making a good impression, as you might imagine. New pastors fall under close scrutiny. It's been a while since I've been a new pastor, but trust me on this. People examine you crosswise, widthwise, lengthwise, upside and downside, and you try to be very careful about what you say and what you do.

After he'd been there just a week or two, my friend went out and bought a new suit. He wanted to look his best when he walked into the sanctuary with his wife and took a seat in one of the front pews. He wanted everyone to know that he was there and on the job. He wanted them to feel good about calling him.

As he sat down near the front, he smiled at the choir, nodded at the senior pastor sitting on the platform, and shook hands with the elderly couple sitting behind him. The service got underway, and my friend felt the tension begin to ebb out of his neck and shoulders. It was nice not to have any "official duties" yet. It was good just to enter into the worship and feel the spirit of the place.

He really didn't notice feeling drowsy until the announcements began.

Quickly he sucked in a deep breath and shifted positions. None of that, now! There was no excuse for drowsiness. But then again…the auditorium *was* stuffy. He glanced longingly at the closed window by the end of the pew, but he couldn't get up and open it without immediately drawing the eyes of everyone in the building. Somehow he was going to have to fight it off this time. He took another deep breath, winked at his wife, flexed his muscles, squared his shoulders, and tried to focus on what the deacon had been saying.

My, what a monotone! Surely they could find someone with a little more rip and zip. This guy's voice reminds me of my fourth period Greek class in Bible school. The one right after lunch. The professor had a voice that droned on and on and on...like the bees in the flowers outside the window...in the spring...bees... flowers...

He caught himself nodding.

This would never do. He could *not* fall asleep! Not in the front row! But my goodness — he was so overcome. He vaguely felt himself sliding sideways into the pew — felt his wife's soft, comforting lap under his head — felt his limbs go numb — felt himself drift away...

Someone clapped. Loud! Once. Twice. Opening his eyes, my friend saw it was the pastor who had clapped his hands — either to make a forceful point or (more likely) to awaken his sleeping associate. It did the trick. He was wide awake now, and realized to his embarrassment that his head was in his wife's lap. Funny...he didn't recognize that dress. Come to think of it, he didn't recognize the woman, either.

It wasn't his wife.

The lap in which he had cradled his head belonged to the lady sitting on the *other* side of him. A lady he'd never seen before. As it turned out, she was a visitor. A woman who had never been to that church before...and never returned!

Peter wrestled with the same kind of problem. Although there is no record of the apostle waking up in someone's lap, the man who became known as "the Rock" slept like a rock through some of the most significant moments in his Lord's ministry. Whether it was at the Mount of Transfiguration or the Garden of Gethsemane, Peter slumbered when he ought to have been alert.

In later years he must have winced as he thought back to those moments. He should have been more vigilant. He should have been praying. He should have been standing for his Lord. *Oh, but his eyelids were SO heavy...*

All of us know what it means to be startled awake...and realize we've been asleep. Most of us know what it's like to wake up and realize we've had our head in the wrong place — for who knows how long! The falling asleep part is bad enough, but waking up is even more humiliating.

- You wake up in class and realize you've been out almost since the opening bell — and people around you are smiling.

- You wake up as the front tires of your car hit the gravel on the shoulder of the highway.

- You wake up in the middle of a conversation and find your friend (or date!) staring at you.

- You wake up and realize your marriage is in serious trouble.

- You wake up and realize your kids have drifted from your

values — and no longer respect what you tell them.

- You wake up and realize you have been foolish with your finances — and may be in too deep to dig back out again.

- You wake up and realize you have neglected to take care of your body — and now you're facing serious health consequences.

- You wake up and realize the Lord has been calling you — insistently, patiently, tenderly calling you — for a very long time.

That's the way it is when you've been drowsing. You rouse up suddenly and say, "My goodness! What time is it? How long have I been asleep? How long have I had my eyes closed? What in the world is going on?" By that time, of course, it may be very late in the game. You will have lost important, irretrievable time. The more you think about what opportunities you have missed through your long period of drowsing, the more shame and humiliation you feel.

A FALL DOWN THE STAIRS

My friend Marc, a missionary in Europe, was sitting in his living room watching television one evening when he heard a horrendous noise that sounded like somebody falling down the stairs! Marc leaped up out of his easy chair and ran over to the stairway. There was his ten-year-old boy, in a heap, on the landing.

Apparently his little guy hadn't been hurt. He wasn't crying, but he *was* talking to himself. And this is what Marc heard him say:

"Oh, you're *so* dumb! You're so stupid. Nobody loves you. No *wonder* nobody loves you! Nobody cares about you. Nobody wants to play with you. Nobody wants to be with you."

Marc was shocked and heartbroken to hear these words. What would possess his child to say such things? He gathered up his little son in his arms and sat with him in the stairwell.

"Son, don't say things like that," Marc chided gently. "It isn't true. People do love you. Hey, falling down happens to everyone. You're not dumb at all. People do want to be with you. They do want to play with you. In fact, Son, I love you very much. *I* want to be with you. I want to spend time with you. And we'll do it. You and me! I'm going to take you fishing. We'll go camping. How does that sound?"

His little boy was crying now. He looked up at Marc and said, "Well, Dad, that's what you told me five years ago."

Marc suddenly felt as though *he* had been the one to fall down the stairs. He felt as though he had been asleep and that he was waking up late — very late — to his failings as a dad.

Marc was startled into awareness. His son had been talking to himself that way because he figured that one of the people who ought to love him most didn't seem to love him at all.

The key, of course, was that when Marc came to that dead end, he did wake up. He did open his eyes. And because of what he saw, he changed courses. Changed his priorities. Changed his schedule. Changed his fathering. From then on, he made sure he had time to do things with his boy. He also made sure that if he promised something, he followed through!

That's the point of dead ends, isn't it? Through various circumstances God brings us up short. His alarm clock rings, drawing us up out of slumber — perhaps a slumber of years. He splashes us with the cold water of realization...

- I need to begin living alertly, with wide opened eyes.
- I need to wake up to my responsibilities.
- I need to wake up to His resources.
- I need to wake up to His calling on my life.
- I need to wake up to my precious opportunities to represent my Lord as a parent, grandparent, husband or wife, brother or sister, neighbor or friend.

Because God loves us, He seeks to wake us up before it's too late. Paul includes the Lord's counsel in his letter to the believers in Ephesus:

> *Therefore He says:*
> > *"Awake, you who sleep,*
> > *Arise from the dead,*
> > *And Christ will give you light."*
>
> Ephesians 5:14

Paul goes on with some specific counsel about "waking up" to our spiritual responsibilities:

> *Be very careful, then, how you live — not as*
> *unwise but as wise, making the most of every*
> *opportunity, because the days are evil. Therefore*
> *do not be foolish, but understand what the*
> *Lord's will is.* (5:15–17, NIV)

The Lord knows how much pain and damage we will have to endure if we continue to sleepwalk through life.

It hurts to wake up and see how much you've missed.

It hurts to wake up and see how much you've lost.

It hurts to wake up and see what might have been.

It hurts to wake up and see how much time has slipped away from you.

And it hurt Peter, too.

SLEEPING ON THE MOUNTAINTOP

One of Peter's first recorded sleeping incidents occurred in a dramatic, never-to-be-repeated incident on a mountaintop. Jesus had told His disciples: "I tell you truly, there are some standing here who shall not taste death till they see the kingdom of God" (Luke 9:27). Those words were fulfilled in a breath-taking way just eight days later. Dr. Luke records it like this:

> *He took Peter, John, and James and went up on*
> *the mountain to pray. And as He prayed, the*
> *appearance of His face was altered, and His*
> *robe became white and glistening. And behold,*
> *two men talked with Him, who were Moses*
> *and Elijah, who appeared in glory and spoke of*
> *His decease which He was about to accomplish*
> *at Jerusalem.* (Luke 9:28–31)

Can you imagine? What an opportunity! What an awe-some privilege! Only three of the twelve disciples were allowed to witness this transformation. And no one in Israel had ever seen anything like it. There was the Son of God, in blinding, heavenly splendor, discussing the most important event of all time with Moses and Elijah (representing the Law and the Prophets). Few men in all of history had been allowed such a divine favor — to listen in to the very counsels of God!

Trouble was, these guys almost slept right through it.

But Peter and those with him were heavy with
sleep; and when they were fully awake, they saw
His glory and the two men who stood with
Him. (Luke 9:32)

I gather from the account that they woke up just as Moses and Elijah were taking their leave of Jesus and returning to heaven. The glory may have already begun to fade. Why had Jesus brought these guys along with Him, anyway? To catch up on their beauty sleep? What had these disciples missed while they slumbered on that mountain, bathed in a pool of heavenly splendor? What words of wisdom had they slept through as Jesus discussed with Moses and Elijah His upcoming death on the cross? Might those words have helped these men cope when that terrible hour came? Might it have kept Peter from denying his Lord? Might it have kept John and James from running away in fear? We won't know until we all meet in heaven.

When Peter finally did awake, he should have repented before the Lord. Instead, he made a belated, clumsy attempt to make up for lost time. He tried to show he was in "full control of the situation" and that it had been prudent of the Lord to bring him along.

*Then it happened, as they were parting from Him,
that Peter said to Jesus, "Master, it is good for us to
be here; and let us make three tabernacles: one for
You, one for Moses, and one for Elijah" — not
knowing what he said. While he was saying this,
a cloud came and overshadowed them; and they
were fearful as they entered the cloud. Then a
voice came out of the cloud, saying, "This is My
beloved Son. Hear Him!" When the voice had
ceased, Jesus was found alone.* (vv. 33–36)

While Peter babbled on about tabernacles and kept assuring everyone how good it was for him to be there, God the Father interrupted with a very important message: "This is My Son. HEAR HIM!" To me, that's just another way of saying, *"WAKE UP! Open your eyes! Open your ears! Listen to what Jesus Christ is saying to you!"*

With an incident like that, you would think Peter had gotten the message. After all, most of us have never been covered by a luminous cloud that drops suddenly out of the sky. Most of us have never heard God's voice booming across a lonely mountaintop. I think if it had happened to me, it might have made a bit of an impression.

And perhaps it did make an impression on Peter. For a while. But not so long after they descended that mountain, he faced an even greater crisis point in his Lord's ministry…and absolutely could not keep his eyes open.

ASLEEP IN THE GARDEN

> *Then they came to a place which was named*
> *Gethsemane; and He said to His disciples, "Sit*
> *here while I pray." And He took Peter, James, and*
> *John with Him, and He began to be troubled*
> *and deeply distressed. Then He said to them, "My*
> *soul is exceedingly sorrowful, even to death. Stay*
> *here and watch." (Mark 14:32–34)*

Once again Peter and the sons of Zebedee were granted an unspeakable privilege. This was the darkest moment thus far in our Lord's life on earth as a man, and the humanity in Jesus longed for the support and love of His closest friends. His request was small enough. "Just watch with Me for a while, won't you, guys? My heart is about to split wide open! I feel so very, very heavy. Won't you be with Me and pray with Me?"

> *He went a little farther, and fell on the ground,*
> *and prayed that if it were possible, the hour*
> *might pass from Him.… Then He came and*
> *found them sleeping, and said to Peter, "Simon,*

are you sleeping? Could you not watch one hour?
Watch and pray, lest you enter into temptation.
The spirit indeed is willing, but the flesh is
weak." (vv. 35–38)

All three men had fallen asleep, but did you notice whom Jesus immediately turned to? *Wake up, Peter! Hang in there with Me, Peter! Don't drop your guard now — of all times, My dear friend!*

But even with these words ringing in their ears, the men turned over and went right back to their dreams.

Again He went away and prayed, and spoke the
same words. And when He returned, He found
them asleep again, for their eyes were heavy; and
they did not know what to answer Him. Then
He came the third time and said to them, "Are
you still sleeping and resting? It is enough! The
hour has come; behold, the Son of Man is being
betrayed into the hands of sinners. Rise, let us be
going. See, My betrayer is at hand." (vv. 39–42)

All the Lord was asking for on that black, horrible night was a little support. A little friendship. A little flash of love. Which, when you think about it, is all that most of the people in our lives are asking for. They're not asking for huge sacrifices or thousand-dollar loans or pints of blood or major commitments of time. They're just asking for a little attention, a little help, a little support, a little prayer, a little bit of encouragement. Maybe a little smile or a loving word now and then.

But it's tough to give those things or even *notice* those needs...if you're asleep.

CALLED INTO COMPANIONSHIP

We might tell ourselves that Peter's "sleeping sickness" was more significant than ours because he failed in his friendship with the Lord Jesus Himself! But is it really so much different for us today? No, Jesus no longer walks the earth as He did then. Scripture tells us He is in heaven at this very hour, sitting at the right hand of His Father. Yet we're also told that — in some mysterious way — we've been called into friendship, into intimate companionship, with God's beloved Son.

Paul puts it this way:

> *God is faithful, by whom you were called into*
> *the fellowship of His Son, Jesus Christ our Lord.*
> (1 Corinthians 1:9)

Another translation renders it like this:

God is trustworthy, through whom you were
called into the companionship *of His Son, our*
Lord Jesus Christ. (MLB)

Called into companionship with God's Son! It's not only a "Lordship" issue with Jesus, it's a *friendship* issue. He is still looking for those who will walk with Him and be near Him and share His heart and concerns. Will we "watch with Him"? Will we pray with Him in the dark hours of the night? Will we put ourselves out at times, and love those whom He loves? When we touch the lives of even "the least of these" in His name, Jesus tells us in Matthew 25 that we are directly ministering to Him. We are showing companionship and friendship to Him.

Yes, Peter was certainly a deep sleeper. Over in Acts chapter 12, a persistent angel had to practically slap him around a jail cell to get him awake and on his feet — and even then he thought he was dreaming! But the important thing is, Peter did finally wake up. And when he came fully awake, he was a mighty instrument in the Lord's hands.

The bottom line isn't whether you've been too drowsy or slept too long. The all-important issue is what you do *after* you wake up! That's everything! Everybody fails…everybody nods off…all of us sleep through priceless opportunities. But what are you going to do when God finally opens your eyes to what's been happening in your life? Turn over and go back to sleep?

What you do when you "wake up" will tell the story of the rest of your life. Are you going to use that dead end as an opportunity to admit your failure, own up to your weakness, your sleepiness, your muzzy-headedness, your lack of discernment, and discover the power of God at work in your life? Or will you just shrug your shoulders and say, "Hey, I'm defeated. I'm stalled right here. I can't advance any further. May as well go back to sleep."

That's why God in His grace brings us to abrupt dead ends in our lives. That's why He speaks to us so gently and firmly when we've been snoozing our way through the days and years of our short lives. He reminds us that we are weak human beings living in a fallen world. We are a people who tend to fall asleep at the wrong times. We get weary. We get discouraged. We get bone tired. We have trouble managing everything on our own. So He waits for us at our dead end and reminds us just how much we need His strength to "redeem the time." We need the energy and power of the Holy Spirit to help us carry on.

And by the way, Peter's untimely naps were no surprise to the Lord. Shortly before the incident in the Garden, Jesus spoke very specifically to His struggling disciple.

"Simon, Simon! Indeed, Satan has asked for
you, that he may sift you as wheat. But I have
prayed for you, that your faith should not fail;
and when you have returned to Me, strengthen
your brethren." (Luke 22:31–32)

Jesus *knew* Peter would fail. He knew he would sleep when he ought to be praying. He knew that His dear friend would deny Him. He knew Satan wanted to shake and worry old Peter like a dog worries a slipper. This man was rumbling along toward a devastating spiritual dead end. Yet Jesus said, "When you have returned to Me, Peter, strengthen your brothers."

And he did!

Filled with the Holy Spirit, Peter stood clear eyed and strong on the day of Pentecost. In the face of prison, beatings, and threats of imminent death, he fearlessly declared the gospel before one and all. Up to the day of his martyrdom, when tradition tells us he was crucified upside down because of his fierce allegiance to Jesus, Peter remembered the lesson of keeping his eyes open.

How do we know that? Just listen to some of these lines from his letters:

Therefore *prepare your minds for action;* be
self-controlled....

Be clear minded and self-controlled so that you can pray....

Be self-controlled and alert. Your enemy the devil prowls around like a roaring lion looking for someone to devour. Resist him, standing firm in the faith....

Therefore, dear friends, since you already know this, *be on your guard....*

1 Peter 1:13; 4:7; 5:8–9; 2 Peter 3:17, NIV

Peter never forgot his experiences of waking up on a dead end. So much so, that he became the apostle of alertness. His stirring calls for spiritual vigilance have echoed down through the millennia. The Lord turned his humiliations into blessings. For all of us.

And by the way, He can do that for you and me, too...if we ask Him.

Have you had any abrupt awakenings lately? Have you found yourself resting and rusting when you ought to have been watching and praying? Have you found your head in the wrong lap or your heart in the wrong pursuits?

Jesus says, "Open your eyes, dear friend. Return to Me. Then go strengthen your brothers!"

Chapter Nine

"LORD, WHAT AM I DOING HERE?"

I remember my first job like it was yesterday.

It was a paper route. But not just any paper route. This was in *Minnesota*.

Minnesota's the state where there's an ice rink on every corner, where cars rust through before they're paid for, and where (if your room is in an unheated attic as mine was), you actually wake up with frost on your eyebrows.

I got up in the chilly house before sunrise, dressed, staggered sleepily down the creaky stairs from the attic, and hauled on boots, knit cap, and heavy coat. Then I stepped outside…sometimes into a howling blizzard. That will open your eyes in a hurry! Every morning I faithfully delivered the *Minneapolis Star* to a large neighborhood near our home. Yes, some of those mornings were brutally cold, but Minnesotans generally learn how to handle that — or move to California. It wasn't the cold that finally did me in.

It was the dogs.

Two dogs in particular seemed to have my number. Through no fault of my own they became my mortal enemies, and I feared them mightily. They resided at the Millers', the little white house on East 86th Street in Bloomington. I'm not sure how this came to be, but it always seemed as though the big houses with yards like football fields had yappy little mouse-dogs, and the little houses had huge, pony-sized dogs who could barely turn around in their tiny front yards.

The Millers had a little house and two big Rottweilers who looked like they'd been raised on a combination of Alpo and Miracle Grow. Every day they hid around the side of the house until I got within range of their chains. Through some secret, prearranged signal, they would both come tearing around the corner at full speed, snarling like a wolf pack around a downed moose. I'm sure it was the big event of their day. They lived for it.

I tried everything to avoid them. Treats, stealth, yelling, snowballs. Nothing helped. But one day, in desperation, I tried a new method...and it almost worked.

Instead of acting terrified, I played it as cool as I could. I walked up to the Miller place like I owned it. I smiled at the side of the house where I knew they lay in wait. I whistled cheerily as I opened the front gate. Right on schedule the dogs came snarling and growling around the corner, expecting to find me in full flight, as usual. They were ready for their daily contest of which one would get to my heels (or the seat of my pants) first.

But on this remarkable morning they found their intended victim calmly waiting for them with a smile on his red-cheeked face. They stopped in their tracks, seemingly abashed and confused.

They looked at each other as if to say, "What's wrong with the kid? He isn't running. He isn't yelling. This is no fun."

"There," I said proudly. "Things are going to be different around here. I'm not afraid of you fellas anymore."

It looked like I was going to pull it off. The Rottweilers seemed discouraged, as if they weren't sure how to proceed or what to do. We stood there looking at each other in a contest of the wills. But then...I was betrayed. A tiny, telltale drop of sweat ran from under my cap, down through my hair, and slid off my left cheek. The dogs looked at me intently, turning their heads this way and that. Then one of them sniffed the air and, with a yelp of pure joy, charged like a bull. I chucked the paper, vaulted the gate, and ran for my life.

From that time on, the Miller dogs owned me.

Never again could I persuade them of my mastery. They had seen — and smelled — my true colors. It was not until I was older that I learned that humans, especially when nervous and perspiring, give off what dog trackers know as a "scent cone," an invisible scent trail which drops off of us and rolls along the ground like an invisible cloud. To the Rottweilers, it was as though I had waved a white flag. And try as I might to look calm and steady, my body chemistry gave me away. The dogs smelled a bluff and answered it with gusto.

I really hated running from dogs. It got even worse after I'd been bitten once or twice. My scent cone kept getting stronger and stronger, emboldening even wimpy little mongrels to join the chase. It was a vicious cycle. The more frightened I became, the more the dogs went after me as an easy mark. And the more they came after me, the more my fear grew.

I finally had to retire at age thirteen and a half, and look for a new line of work. Fortunately, in Minnesota everyone wanted their driveways shoveled about every other day during the winter. Even though I had dead-ended in my news-delivery career, I made the transition to snow shoveling without any severance package, career counseling, golden parachute, or internet job search.

Sure, it's fairly easy to shift on the fly when you're a kid. But the older you get the more difficult those career struggles become.

THE TEST

I'm a preacher now, but there was a time I had strong doubts I'd ever make it. I wanted to please the Lord and felt He was leading me to Bible school. But other than playing college basketball, I had no idea what lay ahead for me.

In the final months of high school, everyone had to take a career placement test. Nowadays they probably do it on computer and give you an instant printout of your future options. But back then you had to answer with pencil and paper what seemed to be hundreds of questions and wait three weeks for the results to be mailed to you. These questions ranged from things like "Do you enjoy being alone?" to "Do you work well with others?" to "How many times a day do you eat?"

I answered them as honestly as I could but vowed I wouldn't let this thing sway me. I already knew I was going to Bible college.

When the results finally arrived, I tore open the envelope and scanned the contents for enlightenment: "You would do best," the counselors told me, "at a job where you are active, physically challenged, and work alone...." They suggested occupations such as forest ranger, fry cook, or steer roper. Although they put forward a number of recommendations and possibilities, they were ironclad about one of their conclusions. I was to stay away from jobs that would put me in direct contact with people. And I was particularly to avoid any occupation that required public speaking. In other words, I could immediately eliminate a career in politics, television, or the ministry.

What a send-off to Bible college! But knowing that God works in mysterious ways, I stayed with my plan and caught a Greyhound for Los Angeles in the fall.

When I arrived on campus, I was so quiet and shy that if you looked me in the eyes my face would turn red. It soon became obvious that I was neither a polished speaker nor blessed with a double portion of charisma.

Through that long freshman year I kept trying to convince myself it was "going to work out somehow." But those test results haunted me. When the studies grew difficult and I had struggled and stumbled through a few in-class sermons, the voice of my doubt grew more and more insistent. *You're only kidding yourself. You'll never be a preacher. You should have been a forest ranger. You should be roping steers in Wyoming or flipping burgers somewhere. What are you doing here?*

I hadn't even begun my career and my ministry, but it already felt like the end.

DEAD-END MINISTRY

As much as my "career potential" seemed limited, I can't imagine what it must have been like for the prophet Isaiah. At his very commissioning service, the Lord told him no one was going to listen to him or pay much attention to him.

Can you imagine? You scrimp and save to go to Bible college or seminary. You study your heart out, taking all the preaching courses you can. Then, just as you're getting ready to graduate, you find this note in your box: "By the way, you will spend the rest of your life preaching, but nobody is ever going to hear you or listen to you. There will be very little response. There will be very few converts. So just do the best you can and try to stay encouraged."

You'd probably do what I would do after receiving a message like that. I'd fall on my knees and say, "O Lord, how long will this be?"

To Isaiah, the answer came back, *It's going to be a long, long time. A lifetime.*

That's the kind of troubling commission the prophet received from the hand of the Lord. But the divine encounter began in a moment of awe, fear, and wonder. Isaiah had a vision of God Himself:

> *In the year that King Uzziah died, I saw the*
> *Lord sitting on a throne, high and lifted up,*
> *and the train of His robe filled the temple.*
> *Above it stood seraphim; each one had six*
> *wings: with two he covered his face, with two he*

covered his feet, and with two he flew. And one
cried to another and said:
> *"Holy, holy, holy is the LORD of hosts;*
> *The whole earth is full of His glory!"*

Isaiah 6:1–3

For the rest of Isaiah's life, that vision burned in his spiritual retinas. His eyes had been filled with the glory of the Lord. And as it turned out, he was going to *need* the memories of that vision through the long days ahead. Just listen to his job description:

And He said, "Go, and tell this people:
> *'Keep on hearing, but do not understand;*
> *Keep on seeing, but do not perceive.'*
> *Make the heart of this people dull,*
> *And their ears heavy,*
> *And shut their eyes;*
> *Lest they see with their eyes,*
> *And hear with their ears,*
> *And understand with their heart,*
> *And return and be healed."*

Isaiah 6:9–10

The prophet-in-training was understandably a little cowed by these gloomy predictions.

Then I said, "Lord, how long?" And He
answered:

> *"Until the cities are laid waste and*
> *without inhabitant,*
> *The houses are without a man,*
> *The land is utterly desolate,*
> *The LORD has removed men far away,*
> *And the forsaken places are many in the*
> *midst of the land."*

vv. 11–12

Isaiah had been called to a task, just as you and I are called to a task. And it wasn't going to be easy. When the people listened to him at all, the best he could expect was unseeing eyes, dull hearts, and heavy ears. What a responsive congregation! He would do the right thing, preach his heart out, and declare God's Word, but there would be no softening, no repenting, no turning, no lasting national revival during his lifetime.

How did he do it? How did he stay on the job year after year, knowing that all he could hope to see would be desolation and ruin? What gave Isaiah the courage to roll out of bed every morning, punch in on God's time clock, and keep plugging away? I believe there were at least two things that gave Isaiah perspective and hope. They are the same things that can give you and me hope when we feel stalled in a dead-end career and ministry.

#1: Go Back to the Vision

Isaiah knew he was a called man. He knew he had been sent by God.

There is great power and confidence in that knowledge.

Whenever he became discouraged and began to waver, he could go back to that time when he saw the Lord, high and lifted up. He could go back to that glorious moment when the angel touched his lips with fire and God commissioned him for service.

The Lord had said, "Who will go?" Isaiah had replied, "Here am I, send me!" And the Lord said, "Go...."

He'd had a revelation, and there wasn't any question about it. God had spoken to him, and he knew what he was supposed to be and do. Memories of divine encounters can sustain you through dry, fruitless seasons. You may forget much of your education, but you'll never forget *revelation*. When you've had an encounter with God, you can't leave it among your old class notes in a box in the attic.

I well remember a particular season in my ministry when I became mired in discouragement. There seemed to be so many problems and heartaches and so few visible results. What was I doing? No good at all! What was the use of sticking with it? I was probably wasting my time, the Lord's time, and everybody else's time.

That's when I decided to take a trip back to Waupaca, Wisconsin.

Now maybe that's not the first place that comes to your mind when you think about getting away for a few days. But it came to my mind right away. Because in that small town there's a little lake. And by that lake there's a Bible camp. And at that Bible camp, when I was still a teen, I met God in a very special way.

We had just listened to a speaker who challenged us to yield our lives fully to Christ and to accept His call into a lifetime of service. I know God spoke to me and called me that day. It wasn't in an audible voice, but to me it was clear. The Lord Jesus was calling Ron Mehl to serve and shepherd His people. And I said, "Here am I, send me."

I said those words on my knees beside a tree in the woods down by the lake. It was very moving and significant to me, and I wanted to do something to remember that day always. So I decided to build a little altar, just like Abraham and Isaac and Jacob built altars to remember where God had met them at different points in their life journeys.

I remember gathering rocks and piling them up behind the tree. I remember tears in my eyes. I remember kneeling and offering myself to Him. I remember the strong sense of His presence.

So I went back. Back to Waupaca. Back to the lake. Back to the little summer camp where God had spoken to me.

I looked for the tree where I had knelt, and found it.

I looked for my little altar, and found it.

I looked again for my calling from God, and I found that, too.

I cleaned some of the moss and dead leaves off of my "memorial stones" and knelt there again, just as I had done so many years before. In a few quiet moments I reminded myself and I reminded the Lord of what had happened in that very place. Whether people thought I was a profound preacher or not didn't really matter. Whether I ever had the privilege to minister to hundreds or thousands of people wasn't the issue either. Whether I would be greatly valued as a pastor and leader wasn't the most important thing.

What really mattered was that God had called me.

He spoke to me. He commissioned me. It was His idea, not mine. It's never been my deal or my design.

Whatever our occupation or calling in life, you and I need to do something like that now and then. We need to go back to those moments when God called us to Himself. We need to go back to those times when we sought Him and He answered us and gave us a job to do. He may have called you to be a plumber, a carpenter, an accountant, a professional athlete, or a church secretary. He may have spoken to you about becoming a godly wife and mother. He may have whispered to you when you were very young in a special church service or at a youth conference. Whatever the task He has given us to do, if we have yielded our lives to Christ and seek to walk in His Spirit, we are *all* in divine service. You as much as me, and I as much as you.

At some point in your journey there may have been a vision — even just a glimpse — of what God wanted for you as His son or daughter. You need to go back to that vision. You need to go back to what God has told you, whether by His Spirit in your heart of hearts or highlighted by His Spirit in the Word of God. You need to cling to the surety of your divine commission when all visible signs before you seem devoid of hope.

I think often of the apostle Paul, languishing in a cold, lonely dungeon somewhere beneath the streets of Rome. I think about him clanking around a filthy cell with a bruising shackle around his ankle. Shortly before his death he wrote these words:

I was appointed a preacher, an apostle, and a
teacher of the Gentiles. For this reason I also
suffer these things; nevertheless I am not
ashamed, for I know whom I have believed
and am persuaded that He is able to keep what
I have committed to Him until that Day.
(2 Timothy 1:11–12)

Paul took that crumpled, blood-stained, tear-stained commission out of his pocket, smoothed it out, and read it again by the light of a flickering oil lamp. Jesus Christ had appointed him! Jesus Christ had sent him! And come what may, the results were in God's hands. The Phillips translation puts verse 12 like this:

For I know the one in whom I have placed my
confidence, and I am perfectly certain that the
work he has committed to me is safe in his
hands until that day.

When Paul looked around him, all he could see were those slimy stone walls. What he *saw* wasn't very encouraging. So he had to continually go back to what God had *said.* He could go back to that day when a bright light — more brilliant and blinding than the noonday sun — knocked him facedown into the desert sand. He could go back to the moment He heard that great voice — strong as thunder, tender with love

— call him by name and enlist him in the King's army.

The light and warmth of those memories kept Paul warm on a cold dead end, just as Isaiah could draw comfort from his own vision.

Do you have a "road to Damascus" in your memory? Is there a Waupaca, Wisconsin, back there somewhere? Is there an "Isaiah encounter," where the Lord seemed very real to you and you were deeply convicted of your sins and your need to follow Him? Do you have a journal entry, a note in your old Bible, or a memory of a time when you shed tears before the Lord and sensed His nearness and direction?

He's the same Lord now that He was then, and He never forgets what He said to you or what you said to Him. Maybe it's time you and God revisited some of those moments... together. Maybe it's time you pulled your divine commission out of the lower drawer of your memory and took another look at it.

But if going back to the vision gave Isaiah encouragement, there was a second thing that helped him endure.

#2: T R U S T   G O D   F O R   L O N G - R A N G E   S U C C E S S

Isaiah had to learn about "the long view" in his ministry. When he was looking for results, he had to borrow God's telescope because there wasn't much close at hand to cheer his heart.

So what do you see in the Book of Isaiah? A lot of telescopic views into the distant future. The prophet certainly saw judgment clouds rolling in, close on the horizon. But beyond that...glorious times were coming! Glad, golden times were ahead.

> *Behold, the Lord GOD shall come with a strong*
> > *hand,*
> *And His arm shall rule for Him;*
> *Behold, His reward is with Him,*
> *And His work before Him.*
> *He will feed His flock like a shepherd;*
> *He will gather the lambs with His arm,*
> *And carry them in His bosom,*
> *And gently lead those who are with young.*
>
> Isaiah 40:10–11

Isaiah knew that God had long-range plans for His people and that they were good plans. And all the while, whether Isaiah could see progress or not, God was working. In the meantime Isaiah needed to stay put. He needed to stay faithful. He needed to work with the flock. He needed to keep people his priority. The reason the Lord had put him there was to be light among men and women, boys and girls.

I can remember times when I have struggled with that "long-term" view of things. My relationship with Jim and his wife, Shirley, who were both alcoholics, comes to mind. I could have so easily given up on them. If it hadn't been for the Holy Spirit's continual prompting, I probably *would* have given up on them.

When I first began pastoring in the Portland area, I learned that one of my expected responsibilities was to take calls from Jim on Friday and Saturday nights. It would mean a drive downtown — at night and sometimes in the rain — to pick him up from a bar, too drunk to drive himself home. I'd put an arm around his shoulder and guide him back to my car. He'd stagger into the passenger seat, and one of several things would happen each time. He'd curse and swear, or he'd want to talk all night. And he was certainly known to throw up, often leaving deposits in my car.

This was like clockwork.

Every weekend you could pretty much plan on the phone ringing with Jim on the other end.

"Passur? Passur, dis ish Jim…"

So off I'd go to pick up Jim. He was a mess. His home was a mess. For that matter, his wife was a mess, too.

But it was a strange thing. I loved Jim. I was a young pastor with just a few people to shepherd, so it was a privilege to look after him. I'd take him home, get him into his house, and get him cleaned up.

Those were days before words like "codependent" were in vogue. All I knew was that Jim was one of my sheep and God had called me to care for him.

But along the way, people would say to me, "Why don't you forget this? It's a waste of time. Why don't you give up on him? Why do you continue to help this guy? You know there's no hope. He's been this way for years."

To be honest, there were times when I'd about "had enough." There were times when I didn't feel like stirring from my warm house and from the company of my wife on a Saturday night. There were times when I wanted to say, "Tell you what, Jim. Why don't you just call a cab and quit getting me out of bed all the time."

But the Holy Spirit hadn't given up on Jim, and He wouldn't let me give up either. He was teaching me that working with people can be a long-term proposition. Not all seeds sprout overnight. Not all trees bear fruit in the first few seasons. Some require cultivation and care for *years*.

Ultimately, even though he remained somewhat of a project, Jim became one of the most faithful men in the church, and a great friend and encouragement to me in my ministry. A trophy of God's persistent grace.

No matter what your occupation or calling in life —
whether you're a pastor, a missionary, or someone who checks
water meters all day — it's people that count. God has you
where you are to touch the lives of those who cross your path.
God has you where you are to hold your light high, like a city
on a hill.

Many of the people I've counseled through the years have
lost their focus and become discouraged because they began
focusing on so many other things. They focused on organiza-
tion, or financial portfolios, or profit and loss, or professional
fulfillment, or climbing the ladder, or on other outward signs
of success. And those things are certainly valid and sometimes
completely necessary.

But you and I can't forget that ultimately — *wherever* we
work, *whatever* we do — God has placed us where we are to
have vital contact with the people around us. And results don't
always happen overnight, in a week, in a year, or even in our
lifetime.

That might mean talking to folks who don't seem responsive, picking up a future deacon out of the gutter, or delivering the Good News to a neighbor in a small house with a very
large Rottweiler.

Go back to the vision. Keep holding out your light. When the King comes in the clouds to call for you, not much else will matter.

Chapter Ten

THE LAST
"AT BAT"

I've already mentioned how I love T-ball games. Did I tell you how they are played?

For those of you who have never had the privilege of seeing this sport of future champions, let me draw you a picture.

Imagine a baseball diamond full of tiny players, pint-sized athletes from the training-wheel set. There is no pitcher or catcher (although players cover these positions for the purpose of fielding). A three-foot plastic pole, cupping a baseball on top, stands next to home plate. The kid who is up to bat simply walks over to the pole and, with his bat, whacks the ball off the top into the field. Then he takes off as fast as his little legs will carry him around the bases while the opposing team scrambles around like puppies chasing the ball. Everything else is played just like baseball (more or less).

Watching T-ball games is fun, funny, heartwarming, and — if you happen to be a pastor — always good for an illustration or two. On my way home from the office one night, I stopped to watch a rousing game at a grade school near the church. This wasn't a practice or a scrimmage. It was a big-time *league* game for these tikes. Intensity was in the air.

A friend in the stands filled me in on the game situation. The visiting team was ahead by nine runs, and the home troops were visibly upset. The left fielder had buried his face in his mitt. The shortstop was tugging nervously at his pants, and both the first and second basemen were crying.

They were "losing bad," and they knew it.

Naturally I looked over at the coach. Would he be tugging at his pants and crying, too? Or would he be the Great Consoler, walking from player to player with a kindly hand and words of fatherly comfort? I was somewhat surprised to see how calm and collected he appeared. He was leaning up against the corner post of the backstop with a bemused expression on his face. He didn't seem mad, upset, or even particularly worried. That just didn't seem natural to me. Didn't he care? Didn't he see how distraught his little warriors had become? Why was he looking so blasé about it all?

As I asked around a bit, I learned something else about T-ball.

Apparently anyone who knows this game is supremely confident of one thing: *The last team at bat always wins.* Why, you ask? It isn't all that complicated. Virtually everyone who steps up to bat gets a hit. (You have to be pretty determined to strike out in T-ball.) And since these little boys and girls aren't particularly accomplished at fielding, all the hits generally end up as runs. So inning by inning, the score surges back and forth, more or less evenly. The first team up in each inning scores a million runs, but the second team, during their turn, answers with a million of their own. And so it goes until the final inning, when the last team up gets the last runs and wins the game.

That's why the coach looked so smug. Let 'em hit, let 'em score, let 'em run around those bases. What did it matter? All his guys had to do was step up, score their quota of runs, and they had the game.

As the visitors padded their lead, the coach walked over to one of the boys who was crying. "Son," he told him, "don't you worry, now. When it's time, you just go up and hit your best. It's gonna be all right." The coach knew something. He wasn't worried. He knew his team had the last "at bat."

That thought comes to mind sometimes when I think about God. No matter what the situation, no matter how dismal, bleak, or useless it seems, God has the last "at bat." He's the scorekeeper, and He's never worried or troubled about the outcome. Nations may rage. People may plot. The kings of the earth and the rulers may take counsel together. But "He who sits in the heavens shall laugh" (Psalm 2:4).

God *will* have the last word, and it will be glorious.

There's a passage in the Book of Isaiah that speaks to a couple of groups in Israel who felt particularly down and out. These men and women felt completely "out of the game." No matter how longingly they looked at the scoreboard, they felt doomed to always be nine runs down in the ninth inning. Listen carefully, for a moment, to the words of the prophet:

> *Do not let the son of the foreigner*
> *Who has joined himself to the LORD*
> *Speak, saying,*
> *"The LORD has utterly separated me from His*
> *people...."*

Isaiah 56:3

At the time those words were written, "foreigners," or Gentiles, were not considered citizens of Israel and were excluded from worship of the Lord. The foreigner looked at his life situation with despair. He knew who the true and living God was. He knew that idols were lifeless hunks of junk, and no gods at all. But he wasn't part of Israel. He felt excluded. Isolated. Separated. Shunned. A second-class citizen. He saw no way that his longings to worship God in His sanctuary could be fulfilled.

There was another group in Israel that felt the same way...or worse.

> *Nor let the eunuch say,*
> *"Here I am, a dry tree."*

v. 3

Eunuchs, too, were perpetual outsiders. Not only did their physical condition keep them from enjoying a wife and children, but they were also prohibited from worshiping with the family of God.

The eunuch felt especially desolate. What he had lost could not be restored. He could look down the long years ahead of him and see no hope. He looked at happy families all around him and could only shake his head and say, "Here I am, a dry tree." *I'm as useless as a dead piece of wood stuck in the ground with no leaves, no blossoms, and no fruit — ever!*

But change was in the wind.

Isaiah unfolded a shocking new aspect within the great plan of God. The One who was called the Servant of the Lord would one day open the door for *everyone* to worship. For *everyone* to draw near. None who turned to the Lord would be excluded! Listen to these words of comfort and hope:

> *For thus says the LORD:*
> *"To the eunuchs who keep My Sabbaths,*
> *And choose what pleases Me,*
> *And hold fast My covenant,*
> *Even to them I will give in My house*
> *And within My walls a place and a name*
> *Better than that of sons and daughters;*
> *I will give them an everlasting name*

That shall not be cut off.
"Also the sons of the foreigner
Who join themselves to the LORD, to serve
Him,
And to love the name of the LORD, to be His
servants...
Even them I will bring to My holy mountain,
And make them joyful in My house of prayer."

Isaiah 56:4–7

There are times in life when any one of us might feel in a dead-end situation. Because of our family background, because of our disabilities, because of our poor health, because of our sin, because of someone else's sin, or just because of events beyond our control, we feel wedged in a no-win situation. The world may regard us as hardly worth notice. Certain people in the family of God may keep us at arm's length. We feel troubled and desolate.

- A divorced individual might feel this way, wherever the fault might lie for the broken marriage.
- A person with a criminal record might feel this way, even though his heart is changed and he wants to follow the Lord.
- A person who has known deep failure might feel this way...failure as a parent, failure as a husband or wife,

failure in school, failure in business, failure on the mission field or in the pastorate.

- A single person who sees no prospects for marriage might feel this way.

- A mentally or physically disabled person might feel this way, as if he or she will never be considered "whole."

In one way or another, at one time or another, we've all felt like "damaged goods." We've all felt like extra furniture, shoved off in some chilly spare room. We see no way out of our situation and conclude that the course of our life has already been decided. Frankly we don't hold onto much hope. It's the ninth inning and there's no chance. Others may win, but we're going to lose.

We find ourselves saying, "I'm just a dry stick. The Lord can't use me." In this passage the Lord speaks very tenderly and says, "Don't call yourself that! You watch and see what I can do with a dry stick. You watch and see what I can do with a life devoted to Me."

When you are walking with God, He has the last "at bat."

When you are joined to Jesus Christ, He has the last word.

He's the Alpha and the Omega, the Beginning and the End. He's the One who decides how things will work out. When you really know and understand that — holding onto the reality of that truth with all that's in you — a sense of confidence rises in your heart. Confidence the world can never understand, imitate, or manufacture.

Did you note what He said to the eunuchs?

"Even to them I will give in My house
And within My walls a place and a name
Better than that of sons and daughters;
I will give them an everlasting name
That shall not be cut off."

In other words there is that which endures longer than a physical family. There is a name more sure than a family name. There are blessings even richer than the blessing of sons and daughters. The eunuchs who put their trust in God would find all their hearts' desire in Him. They would find "a place and a name" within His walls.

Isaiah foresaw a day when Jesus would open the way for everyone and anyone to approach God through the blood of His cross. To underline that wonder…guess who the Holy Spirit sought out as the very first recorded convert to Christianity from the continent of Africa?

An Ethiopian eunuch (Acts 8:26–39).

That "dry stick" planted in African soil became a fragrant, blossoming tree, bearing the fruit of life for generations. God has the last word about the tools He chooses to use.

SOME FAMOUS "AT BATS"

I think of other people in Scripture who were low on runs in the ninth inning.

- ‑ Rahab the harlot may not have had a good self-image. She knew who she was, and she knew what she'd done and how she'd lived. Her adult life was a parade of face-less men in dark rooms over endless, weary nights. And what's more, her whole city was now marked for destruc-tion. What chance did she have? Yet when the opportu-nity came, she placed her faith in the God of Israel and found deliverance and a new life among His people. Ultimately she became part of the royal lineage that birthed David, Solomon, Hezekiah, Josiah…and the Lord Jesus Christ. God had the last at bat.

- ‑ I think of Gideon, a timid, amateur general who found himself with three hundred unsoldierly farmers facing an invading army so vast it couldn't be numbered. Gideon was well aware of the scoreboard. He didn't need to listen to play-by-play on the radio to know he was down by a bundle and in deadly trouble. He didn't need to read the odds in the morning paper. Yet when the smoke cleared the next day, Gideon's team was utterly victorious. The Midi-anites hadn't counted on God stepping up to the plate.

- Elisha's servant, Gehazi, got up one morning to see the hills around the city crawling with enemy troops. Stumbling into the house in a terrible panic, he wailed, "Alas, my master! What shall we do?"

> *[Elisha] answered, "Do not fear, for those who are with us are more than those who are with them." And Elisha prayed, and said, "Lord, I pray, open his eyes that he may see." Then the Lord opened the eyes of the young man, and he saw. And behold, the mountain was full of horses and chariots of fire all around Elisha.*
> (2 Kings 6:16–17)

The enemy forces were impressive and frightening, and they had Elisha and Gehazi surrounded. But they weren't going to have the last word. God's forces were even more impressive and frightening, and they had the *enemy* surrounded!

Like Gehazi, we're all tempted to take a Polaroid snapshot of our life circumstances and hold it up as evidence that there's no hope. But life on earth is not a snapshot; it's a motion picture. *And no one has seen the end of the movie yet!* When the credits roll at the end of time, we'll understand that the One who is both Producer and Director has been in control of every frame.

The Checkers Champ

I've never been patient enough for chess, but at different times in my life I've considered myself quite a checkers player.

Back in a day when it was cool to play checkers, I knew I could whip about anyone in my youth group. I hate to admit it, but I got a little cocky about it. No, you couldn't letter in checkers, but being the undisputed church champ went to my head a bit.

I remember a day when I had just beaten my best friend, Roy Hicks Jr.

He shook his head and grinned. "Gee, Ron, you're sure good at checkers."

"Yeah, I guess I really am," I said modestly.

I was feeling so good about myself I didn't notice the little glint in Roy's eye. He was setting me up, and I didn't even know it. "Well, gosh, Ron. You know, you should play my dad sometime. He's pretty good at checkers. I'm sure *you* can beat him but…well, it might be a good game."

I swallowed Roy's bait like a gullible trout.

So the next time I saw Dr. Roy Hicks Sr., I said, "You know, I'm the checkers champ of my youth group, and I hear you're pretty good. I'd like to challenge you to a friendly game, if you'd like."

I tried to sound casual about it. Not overconfident. But I

knew I was good, and I couldn't wait to demonstrate my prowess.

"Well sure, son," Dr. Hicks replied. "I'd love to play. But then…I haven't played in years."

That, I figured, was an old person's way of excusing his losing before we even began the game. Oh, this was going to be *rich*.

I was, however, a little worried about Roy Jr. I knew how he loved and respected his dad, and I thought it might hurt his feelings if I embarrassed the man. On the other hand, *he* had been the one who suggested the match, not me.

As Dr. Hicks and I sat down to play, Roy Jr. looked at me and grinned. (But what was he smiling about?) Hindsight tells me he had been through this himself.

I set up the board. There was something about the way Dr. Hicks cracked his knuckles that bothered me a little. It was almost as if he relished this contest. Didn't he know who he was up against?

I went to work right away in my best attack style. I jumped one of his lead guys, and he sat back and rubbed his chin for a moment. I thought, *Boy, this guy's old and rusty. Probably slowing down a little. Probably doesn't know anything about modern checkers strategies. Probably played with bottle caps or buttons in his day.*

The game went on, and I jumped here and there, thinning my opponent's ranks rather rapidly. I shot a quick look at Roy Jr. to gauge his disappointment at the demise of his hero.

Inexplicably my friend had something that resembled a smirk on his face.

At that point I felt supremely confident about the game. Really I was just toying with him. I needed to go for the kill and put him out of his misery. I looked up at Dr. Hicks and was surprised to see the tiniest hint of a smile touching the corners of his mouth. It bothered me a little because I was wiping him off the board. He should have looked more chastened and subdued.

We played until he had only three or four checkers left, while my offensive machine was largely intact and rolling.

Suddenly Dr. Hicks looked up at me and said, "Son, are you *sure* you want to move there?"

What was he trying to do? Shake my confidence? Break my concentration? It was the oldest trick in the book and didn't seem worthy of Dr. Hicks. It certainly wouldn't worry the likes of me. I quickly surveyed my last couple of moves and determined them to be good ones. "Yes sir," I said quietly. "It's your move."

I had never seen one checker jump so many times. Jump,

jump, jump, jump, jump. In a single move, he almost cleared one side of the board.

"King me," he said.

In the end, of course, he destroyed me, and Roy Jr. laughed his head off. I'll never forget that drubbing. What I learned that day was that a good checkers player never minds losing a checker or two along the way…as long as he knows he's going to win in the end. And Dr. Hicks *knew*. He was a master, and *he* was the one who had been toying with *me*.

King David wasn't a checkers player, but what he learned observing life wasn't much different from what Dr. Hicks taught me on those red-and-black squares.

> *Wait on the LORD,*
> *And keep His way,*
> *And He shall exalt you to inherit the land;*
> *When the wicked are cut off, you shall see it.*
>
> Psalm 37:34

In other words, "It ain't over 'til it's over!" The way things are now are not the way things will be. The way life circumstances appear at this particular moment may be very misleading and deceptive. He goes on to explain.

> *I have seen the wicked in great power,*
> *And spreading himself like a native green tree.*

Yet he passed away, and behold, he was no more.
Indeed I sought him, but he could not be found.

(vv. 35–36)

David knew what it was like to lose a lot of checkers to proud, fierce opponents. It looked as if he couldn't win and they couldn't lose. Yet after a season of setbacks and deep distress, it was David wearing the crown! He went on to declare,

But the salvation of the righteous is from the
  LORD;
He is their strength in the time of trouble.
And the LORD shall help and deliver them;
He shall deliver them from the wicked,
And save them,
Because they trust in Him.

(vv. 39–40)

David is saying, "Don't be fooled by externals. Don't be discouraged by the way circumstances seem to be crowding you right off the board. Just remember that when God gets *His* turn, everything changes."

Whether the game is checkers, T-ball, or life on a dysfunctional planet, this Coach isn't nervous. He *knows.* There's no doubt about the outcome of the contest. Even when the world would point at the scoreboard and laugh us right off the field, He invites us to step up to the plate and swing.

If you could only imagine the smile on God's face, it would speak volumes.

"Don't give up, My son. Don't cry, My daughter, and don't you worry now. When it's time, you just go up and hit your best. The game is already ours."

In other words, He who bats last wins the game.

Chapter Eleven

THE MARK
OF THE
KING

B ob had systematically worked his way to the back of the garage and was about to make his exit when he first saw it.

Although partially hidden underneath a tablecloth and an old comforter, the shape was unmistakable. It was a motor-cycle. And not only that…it was a Harley.

Obviously it wasn't part of the garage sale, and that piqued Bob's interest.

"Is the bike for sale?" he asked the homeowner.

The man shrugged. "Well…don't rightly see why not. The wife says it's all got to go. But I'll warn ya. That bike hasn't run since I've had it. Motor's seized up. Won't turn over. Could probably buy yourself a new one with what it'd cost to fix up that old thing."

Bob nodded patiently. "All the same, how much do you want for it?"

"I'm sure they'd give me thirty-five bucks for the metal at the scrap yard. How does that sound?"

Bob looked at the rusty old heap. What would his wife say if he brought it home? But still…to a practiced eye, it had potential. Even if it didn't run, he could get it shined up as a con-versation piece. And he could surely sell it again for more than thirty-five dollars. Parts alone would be worth more than that.

"Okay," he said. "I'll give you the thirty-five. Can I pick it up tomorrow?"

Bob was an avid garage-sale enthusiast. Every Saturday morning he made it a hobby to cruise the streets, avenues, and cul-de-sacs of Downey, California, and hit as many sales as he could. There was always the off chance that on one golden Saturday he would lay his hands on the elusive "great treasure" for which he had been searching for years. What would his wife say *then* about "wasting time and money on other people's junk"?

On a typical Saturday not long ago, Bob was up with the birds, had his newspapers marked, his addresses listed, and was out of the house and on the hunt while most of Downey was still asleep. By 10:30 or 11:00 A.M., he was returning home with a few, newly acquired prizes. He had time to stop at one more address. But should he? Yes, he would stop briefly, even though prime shopping hours were over.

At that last stop, in the back of the last garage, he saw the bike.

Shortly thereafter the old Harley was occupying space in Bob's garage. After a few weeks of procrastinating, he finally got around to calling Harley-Davidson, just to see what a few of the major parts for restoration would run him. He connected with someone on the parts line and asked a few questions.

"Why don't you give me the serial number," the dealer said, "and I can look that up for you."

Bob gave him the number.

"Hold on just a second while I look it up."

Bob waited on hold, listening to a sixties rock station piped into the receiver. *How appropriate,* he thought. After what seemed an inordinately long time, the parts man returned to the line. And just in time. One more number by the Trogs or Country Joe and the Fish might have driven Bob off the line altogether.

Somehow the Harley man sounded different. Strange. Self-conscious. Like something was up.

"Uh, sir...I'm going to have to call you back, okay? Could I get your full name, address, and phone number, please?"

Why does he need my name and address? Bob wondered. But then again, what was the harm? It was no big deal. He'd probably end up on some motorcycle mailing list. Bob gave the man what he wanted and hung up.

After a few minutes, however, he found himself getting nervous. He regretted giving information about himself over the phone. *What if the bike had been involved in a crime of some sort? What if drugs were involved — or murder? What if the bike was stolen? Was he in danger of prosecution? Maybe the police were already on their way — or a Hell's Angel, ready to reclaim his bike and rearrange Bob's face.*

Bob sweated for a couple of days without hearing back from Harley. But just as his worries were beginning to subside, the phone rang. This time, however, it wasn't the parts man; Bob found himself talking to a Harley executive. The man seemed overly friendly, making Bob feel even more uneasy.

"Listen, Bob," said the man, "I want you to do something for me, okay?"

"Umm. Well, I guess."

"Bob, I want you just to set the receiver down — don't hang up — and take the seat off your bike and see if anything is written underneath. Would you do that for me, Bob?" The man talked like an air traffic controller bringing in an off-course 737.

And Bob felt like he was about to hit wind shear.

But he grabbed a screwdriver, did as he was told, and returned to the phone. "Yes," he said, "it does have something written there. It's engraved, and it says, 'THE KING.' Listen, is there some kind of trouble here? What's this all about?"

There was a moment or two of profound silence on the other end. Bob felt like the man on the long distance commercial listening for a pin to drop.

"Bob, my boss has authorized me to offer you $300,000 for the bike, payable to you immediately. How about it? Do we have a deal?"

Bob was so stunned he could hardly speak. "I–I'll have to think about it," he stammered. He hung up the phone and let himself slump slowly to a sitting position on the kitchen floor.

The next day Bob got a call from Jay Leno, the late-night television talk sultan. Leno explained that "he had a thing about Harleys" and offered Bob $500,000.

"The King," of course, was none other than Elvis Presley. The serial number had made that clear, and the engraved legend under the seat had removed all doubt. The bike Bob had redeemed from the scrap pile for thirty-five dollars had once been owned by "The King of Rock 'n Roll." And it was worth half a million — *at the least*. After all those years of seeking "The Big Find," Bob finally found it. But he hadn't even recognized what he had.

It goes to show you that truly one man's junk is another man's treasure. The value of the motorcycle, of course, wasn't in the metal or the parts. It didn't even run! The value had nothing to do with the bike's beauty, what it was made of, or how well it performed. Where was the value then? It was all tied to the fact that it had been owned by "the King." He had touched it, ridden it, taken pride in it. And the inexplicable value our culture has attached to Elvis Presley — approaching deity status — transferred to his motorcycle. There were people willing to pay a small fortune for the privilege of saying, "I own Elvis Presley's motorcycle."

Bob didn't realize he had something of great value. He hadn't a clue about the bike's previous owner. He just saw something cheap on the marketplace — an opportunity for a little profit. What he found out, of course, was that ownership was by far the most important truth about that old Harley. In fact, ownership was *everything*.

And what is it that speaks most forcefully about your value and mine?

Is it what we're made of? Is it based on our job title or economic status? Is it determined by what we can do and how we "perform"?

SMALL VALUE

I remember a day I was sitting in my office, feeling particularly useless. I've forgotten what had caused me to feel that way. It may have simply been a blue Monday after an intense Sunday. For whatever reason, that's the dead end where I found myself parked that morning. I felt about as valuable as a canary-yellow, three-dollar bill and was leafing through things on my desk for possible sources of encouragement. What I finally picked up to read, however, didn't help me at all.

Someone had sent me a little study on the "value" of the human body. What a cheerful item! I think the grand total for all the ingredients came to a little over a buck.

Apparently there is enough lime in the body to whitewash one chicken coop. (There's life purpose for you!) There's enough potassium to fire one toy cannon. Enough sulfur to rid one dog of fleas. Enough fat for one medium bar of soap. Enough phosphorous to make three matches. Enough iron to make a twelve-penny nail. Enough gas to fill a quart jar. And there's water, too, of course. But water's free.

Where, then, is my value? If all of the ingredients of my physical body are worth about the same as a cup of bad coffee, what keeps me from feeling worthless?

Does it depend on what I can *do?* I have some gifting and training to do certain things. And so do you. If I didn't have my present job, I could earn a living doing something else. Work is honorable, and I have the two hands God has given me to perform certain tasks that are more or less valuable to other people.

But what if I *lost* both of my hands in an accident, like the man I described in chapter seven? What would I be worth then? And what about my mom, who after multiple strokes was left unable to speak or to walk? Was she any less valuable to me? What if I was afflicted with Alzheimer's disease and lost most of my memories? What if I had a mental illness that put me in the state hospital? What if I had been born as a Down syndrome baby? Would my value be less? Would I be less important?

What brings such great value to our lives isn't what we're made of or what we look like or what our IQ might be or what we can accomplish. What gives me a sense of worth and significance is that I belong to God. I have been redeemed by God's own Son at great suffering and great price. He owns me. He lives within me. He's touched me in so many ways. And *nothing* can change that. Nothing can separate me from the love of God, which is in Christ Jesus my Lord.

Someone once said that Americans know the price of everything and the value of nothing. In our country a Van Gogh painting sold for $82.5 million, a baseball card sold for $100,000, a sports car went for $295,000, and a basketball player signed a ten-year contract for $87 million.

Yet while we place such high value on the temporal and the trivial, what causes men and women to kill handicapped or unwanted babies while they're still in their mothers' wombs? They don't understand or won't acknowledge the inestimable value God places on those babies.

What causes a young woman to go off to college and give herself away to the first guy who comes along with a fast car and a line of baloney? She doesn't understand her priceless value. She will do anything and give herself to anyone to make herself feel valuable and treasured…even if only for a night.

Jesus spoke very clearly to the issue of personal value. But He did it in a way no one expected or had probably ever heard before. For His object lessons, He spoke about birds and hair.

The Price of Sparrows

Sparrows were the first-century equivalent of snack food. In New Testament times people didn't have potato chips, pretzels, buffalo wings, or Snicker's bars. But they did have vendors around the Temple in Jerusalem selling crunchy, roasted sparrows, and I guess that was adequate. I've never tried one myself, so I can't really make a comparison.

Whatever you might think about the culinary use of sparrows, they were plentiful and cheap. And as the Lord Jesus did so often in His ministry, He took a common object from everyday life and employed it to make a point. Here is what He said:

> *Are not two sparrows sold for a penny? Yet not one*
> *of them will fall to the ground apart from the will*

of your Father. And even the very hairs of your
head are all numbered. So don't be afraid; you
are worth more than many sparrows.
(Matthew 10:29–31, NIV)

In the gospel of Luke He said:

Are not five sparrows sold for two pennies? Yet not
one of them is forgotten by God. (Luke 12:6, NIV)

Did you notice the variation in prices? In Matthew, they were sold two for one penny. In Luke, Jesus says they're sold five for two pennies.

I'm not a mathematician, but I know that if you can buy two sparrows for a penny, you ought to get four sparrows for two pennies. Why the discrepancy? I think this simply reveals what a small value that culture placed on those birds. Two for a penny here, four or five for two pennies there, what does it matter? They're just dumb little birds. Who cares about a sparrow? We'll throw in an extra one at no charge.

Yet God says, "I know when every bird falls from a tree. There isn't a sparrow in the history of the earth that has escaped My notice."

Who cares? God cares.

Who's counting? God's counting.

Now if He watches with great concern the comings and

goings of a sparrow, then how much more does He value your life and mine?

In the same passage Jesus affirmed that every hair on our head is numbered.

I heard someone say, regarding this passage, that blondes have the most hairs with 145,000. Brunettes are second with 120,000. And redheads come in last with 90,000. Who keeps track of such trivia, you ask? God does. From His point of view, each hair has its own personalized, individual number. He knows when number 587 comes out in your brush. He sees number 132,401 when it slides down the drain.

Why does He choose to know such things? Well, it's really no problem; He just knows *everything*. Yet Jesus used this illustration to drive home a point: No matter what value anyone else may place on you or me, God is deeply interested in and concerned about every detail of our lives, and He values us highly. How highly does He value you? You were worth a Son to Him. As Paul said:

> *What then shall we say to these things? If God is*
> *for us, who can be against us? He who did not*
> *spare His own Son, but delivered Him up for us*

all, how shall He not with Him also freely give
us all things? (Romans 8:31–32)

I love Bill and Gloria Gaither's song that says, "But the One who knows me best loves me most." He knows everything I've done, everything I've said, and everywhere I've been, but He still loves me. If no one else values me, He values me. If no one else cares whether I live or die, God cares profoundly. David recognized this when he wrote:

> *When my father and my mother forsake me,*
> *then the LORD will take me up.*
>
> Psalm 27:10, KJV

Is my value less if I am rejected by my father and mother… by my children…by my spouse…by my own brothers and sisters? No. Even though those things would bring me great sorrow and grief, my value is not set by anyone other than God. I am treasured by My Creator and Savior, and that is the truth that will endure forever. Peter reminds us that…

> *Ye are a chosen generation, a royal priesthood,*
> *an holy nation, a peculiar people; that ye should*
> *shew forth the praises of him who hath called*
> *you out of darkness into his marvellous light.*
> (1 Peter 2:9, KJV)

I used to think the word "peculiar" meant just that. In

other words, to be a Christian you had to be a little weird, dress funny, and act a bit strange. But a closer look at the King James term "peculiar" reveals its true meaning. We are a private, special, treasured possession of God. We're *privately owned.* Purchased by Him. His mark and seal are upon us. We, too, are engraved with the words "The King."

TOKEN LOVE

I didn't know what a dangerous pronouncement I had just made.

"We will *never* have a dog in this household."

There wasn't anything wrong with the pronouncement. It had the weight of logic and sanity behind it. As far as pronouncements go, it was really pretty good.

It's just that I hadn't met Token before.

When my wife and young sons came home one day with a tiny, reddish brown Pomeranian puppy, they told me it was "just for the night. We'll take him back to the store in the morning."

Yeah, right.

Once he started licking faces and tugging at shoelaces and acting so happy to have found a home and people to love him... well, it was all over. My pronouncement was out the window.

Our sons named the puppy "Token." Because of what I'd said, I guess they figured the family could never have a *real* dog, so this one was only a "token dog." Whether he was "token" or not, he soon became an indispensable member of the Mehl household, and everybody fell in love with him. For a dog, he had amazing discernment. He knew who to butter up and when. He knew who would likely enforce the rules and who would just talk about enforcing the rules — and how to handle both of them. He dutifully barked at strangers and pretended to be fierce, but it was all show. He really wouldn't harm a fly.

I have no idea how one little dog could so take over a family's affections. I'd heard of it happening but had never experienced the actual phenomenon. After all, I was the "no dog" guy. But there was no denying it; Token was loved, and he knew it. He didn't need any pedigree certificates or championship trophies — or a college degree, for that matter. This wasn't a logic thing; it was love.

When Token had been with us for a little more than a year, he came in from the backyard one afternoon, and we noticed he was limping a little. A thorn maybe? Surely he hadn't been fighting! Joyce examined his legs and paws but couldn't see anything wrong. Yet Token continued to limp. When we saw he couldn't jump up on the couch anymore to watch TV with us, we knew that something would have to be done.

We took him to the vet, not realizing that this would begin a series of many, many such visits over a period of years. It turned out Token had severe problems in both knees. He ended up having three surgeries to correct the problem. It alleviated some of the pain, but he still limped.

Next came the hip. Dysplasia, an ugly word in dog circles. More surgeries followed.

After that, he began to suffer with a problem in the vertebrae of his neck. Surgery again!

Little dogs are supposed to be bouncy and vivacious, but Token couldn't manage it anymore. The will was there, but the little body wouldn't cooperate. He had trouble getting around.

The problems with his joints would have been bad enough, but it got worse. A lot worse. Token had a skin disease, and before long, big chunks of his coppery fur began to fall out, leaving patches of bare skin and open sores. In order to treat him, we had to clip even more of his fur, right down to the skin. Have you ever seen what a Pomeranian looks like under all that fur? Frankly, there isn't much there. It's pretty pitiful, and you have to look twice to make sure you're looking at a dog and not — well, something else.

Token was a mess. His once-proud mane was chopped and mutilated. He looked terrible. If you had put one hundred dogs in a row and ranked them for attractiveness or desirability, Token would have been Number 101.

The funny thing was, he seemed to *know* he was ugly. He looked ashamed or embarrassed somehow. He cowered when you stooped to pet him. He would slink around the house, looking up at you as if to say, *This is terrible. I can't believe this is happening to me. I wouldn't blame you if you didn't pet me or talk to me.*

Someone in the Bible named their son "Ichabod," during a time of Israel's national disgrace. The name means "the glory has departed." Poor Token was Ichabod all over, and somehow he knew it.

I can still see Joyce sitting on the floor, rubbing salve into Token's sores. He would stand there and take it, trembling a little and trying every now and then to lick her hand. As ugly as he was, he still seemed beautiful to us. No, it doesn't make any sense. But as I said, this wasn't logic; it was love.

Somewhere along the line, when he was at his worst, he must have gained the perspective that we loved him. I don't know how this works with dogs or how to explain it. He just knew he was loved, that's all. And when you know that — really *know* that in your heart of hearts — it makes all the difference in your life. You're able to face trials and tribulations you might not otherwise be able to bear.

If you've never loved a dog and been loved by a dog, this probably isn't making much sense to you. You're probably saying, "For pity's sake, why didn't they just put the poor thing to sleep and take it out of its misery?" As a matter of fact, a number of people did say that to us — and not always very subtly. But it wasn't that simple. Token had given us his full measure of devotion, and as long as there was a chance of his getting better, we wanted to do what we could for him.

When Token was about twelve years old, the vet sat down with us in his office. He knew how difficult it had been to care for Token, especially in his declining years. As painful as the decision was, we all agreed that Dr. Labavitch should take him home and work with him for a while. He said, "Token needs lots of special attention. Our kids will love him, and I can give him the extra treatment he needs. Why don't we give it a try?"

As it turned out, Token did very well under the vet's care and supervision. As of this writing, he's still alive and happy with his new family. No, he's not jumping through hoops or chasing sports cars around the block, but he's getting on fine for an elderly Pomeranian. Watching him reminds me of an old, retired linebacker. A little hobbled, but still with plenty of fire, zest, and good humor.

That's a nice story with a happy ending, but I'd like to add something here.

Token is just a *dog*. Just an animal. His value doesn't even deserve mention in the same breath with the value of a human being — an eternal, living soul. Yes, we loved and cared for that little dog, even when he was hurt and unlovely, just as God cares for humble little sparrows.

But the Son of God didn't die for dogs and sparrows. He died for wounded, unlovely people like you and me. While we were still sinners and rebels against God, He died a criminal's death, carried our sins, and endured an agony of separation from His Father beyond anything that can be put into words.

There is no greater expression of value than that. What more could He possibly say or do than what He has said and what He has done? There is no room for doubt. We may feel worthless from time to time, but our value has been established beyond question.

The world may never see it that way of course. The world might try to sell you on the cheap, or consign you to the back of a dusty garage and cover you up with an old tablecloth. But that doesn't matter. If you know Jesus Christ as Savior and Lord, the truth will come out eventually. Your true value will be known before men and angels.

No one argues with the mark of the King.

Chapter Twelve

THE FINAL DEAD END

I began this book with the story of my young friend Jonah, a teenager who fell nine hundred feet down the face of Mt. Jefferson and ended up in a broken, bloody heap at the bottom of an icy crevasse.

It was certainly the worst and darkest dead end of his life. But Jonah not only walked away from that experience, he walked away with several truths burning in his heart —truths his pastor hopes he never, never forgets.

- No matter how far you fall, you cannot fall out of the reach of God's hand.

- No matter how difficult your circumstances, heaven has resources that can see you through.

- No matter how dark and hopeless your dead end, God will provide light to show you the way…if only you will open your eyes to see it.

Has anyone, anywhere, dropped as far as Jonah and lived to tell the story?

Yes. There was one.

When the Son of God stepped from the shining pinnacle of heaven's glory, He plunged much farther than nine hundred feet. He came down a long way. A very, very long way. No one pushed Him over the edge. He didn't slip or stumble. He didn't lose His grip and fall into an uncontrolled slide. He stepped willingly from the warmth and joy of the highest place, knowing well what awaited Him at the bottom.

Ridicule. Humiliation. Deprivation. Rejection. Stress. Hatred. Betrayal. A cross. Unspeakable suffering. God's fiery wrath. Separation from His Father. Death.

Paul says this:

> *Christ Jesus: Who, being in very nature God,*
> *did not consider equality with God something*
> *to be grasped, but made himself nothing, taking*
> *the very nature of a servant, being made in*
> *human likeness. And being found in appearance*
> *as a man, he humbled himself and became obe-*
> *dient to death — even death on a cross!*
> (Philippians 2:5–8, NIV)

That's a long way down the mountain.

And in the bottom of that dark crevasse — a black canyon created by my sin and your sin — His body was bruised and broken and torn.

It was dark. It was lonely. He was thirsty. He was naked. He was in terrible pain and distress. His friends had scattered. His lifeblood was ebbing away. He called out in the darkness, but there was no rescue for Him. Everyone had forsaken Him. Even His Father.

Men jeered at Him. His enemies laughed. Demons danced and rejoiced. Death came slowly and closed its hand around His heart.

Why did He do it? Why did He step off that beautiful mountaintop and fall into such terrible darkness? Why did He walk so willingly down that dead-end road, knowing what waited Him there?

Why did He do it?

He did it so that you and I would never, never have to do it ourselves. He went all the way down that final dead end, a road dropping off into hell and the abyss, so that we would never have to fall off that edge and be lost. We were headed in that direction! Hell was our destination, our final stop, and that's where every one of us would have ended up.

But look! He stands in the middle of that dead end, with His arms outstretched, turning us back from eternal death, eternal darkness, and separation from God.

Not long ago California's San Joaquin Valley was shaken by a powerful earthquake — a tremor strong enough to buckle roads and move buildings off their foundations. Near the little town of Coalinga a bridge over Interstate 5 collapsed in the night. Highway patrolmen quickly sealed off the roads with barricades to stop traffic and turn people back from the deadly danger.

But not everyone took those warnings seriously. One couple in a minivan approached the roadblock in the darkness. The barricades must have been very clear in their headlights. As near as anyone can tell, they stopped, then deliberately drove *around* the warning signs and plunged to their deaths in the canyon that yawned ahead.

Who knows what they were thinking? That the barricades were there by mistake? That the situation really wasn't serious? That the warning signs applied to others but not to them? That whatever lay ahead of them that night was somehow "more important" and "worth the risk"?

We'll never know. All we know is that their tire tracks led around the row of barricades and straight off the edge of the shattered bridge. In the second or two when their tires left solid ground and they hung in empty space, they must have realized their mistake. But it was too late.

And that, I believe, is the only way to hell.

You have to drive around Jesus Christ.

You have to close your ears to His warnings.

You have to close your eyes to His cross.

You have to close your heart to His great love.

You have to reject the price He paid to buy you back from Satan's slave market.

You have to go right around the barricades, step on the

accelerator, and hurl yourself into the darkness.

But you *don't* have to. Instead of running from God's Son, you can run right into His embrace. The two thieves, crucified on either side of Jesus Christ, came to death's dead end at the same time He did. They saw the darkness, they felt the earthquake, they saw the road ahead dropping off into empty space. One looked right at Jesus Christ and flung words of hatred and rejection into His bleeding face. The other looked at Jesus and — close as he was to hell and the edge of the cliff — called out for mercy.

> *Then he said to Jesus, "Lord, remember me when*
> *You come into Your kingdom." And Jesus said to*
> *him, "Assuredly, I say to you, today you will be*
> *with Me in Paradise."* (Luke 23:42–43)

Isn't it amazing? That dying thief had *one chance* to repent before he died and passed into eternity. And Who do you think happened to be right beside him, with words of comfort, hope, and salvation?

The Son of God. The Savior. The One who came to "seek and to save what was lost."

That's always the way it is. Jesus reveals Himself right where He is needed most. Not on the top of the mountain, but at the bottom. Not on a pinnacle, but in a crevasse. Not in a castle, but in a manger. Not on a throne, but on a cross.

Not on some sunny, landscaped parkway, but on a lonely dead end in the dark of night.

What happens when you meet Jesus Christ?

You meet God at a dead end.

Jesus Himself, standing in the shadow of His cross, said:

> *"Most assuredly, I say to you, he who hears My word and believes in Him who sent Me has everlasting life, and shall not come into judgment, but has passed from death into life."*
> (John 5:24)

In other words, for those two thieves who were only a few heartbeats away from eternity, the warning sign of all warning signs at that darkest dead end was Jesus with His arms outstretched to turn them away from death and point them toward heaven.

With God, there really are no dead ends.

Bumps in the road, yes. Inconveniences, for sure. A fall here and there.

But God always makes a way.

When you meet Jesus Christ and receive Him, you'll have not only turned back from destruction, you'll have found the only bridge into heaven and eternal life. It's all because of Him.

How does that old song go? *Hallelujah, what a Savior!*